SELLING
THE WAY YOUR
CUSTOMER
BUYS

MARVIN C. SADOVSKY
& JON CASWELL

SELLING THE WAY YOUR CUSTOMER BUYS

Understand Your Prospects' Unspoken Needs & Close Every Sale

amacom

American Management Association

New • York • Atlanta • Boston • Chicago • Kansas City • San Francisco • Washington, D.C.
Brussels • Mexico City • Tokyo • Toronto

This publication is designed to provide accurate and authoritative information in regard to the subject matter covered. It is sold with the understanding that the publisher is not engaged in rendering legal, accounting, or other professional service. If legal advice or other expert assistance is required, the services of a competent professional person should be sought.

Library of Congress Cataloging-in-Publication Data

Sadovsky, Marvin C.
    Selling the way your customer buys : understand your prospects'
unspoken needs & close every sale / Marvin C. Sadovsky & Jon
Caswell.
      p.   cm.
    Includes bibliographical references and index.
    ISBN 0-8144-7889-1
    1. Selling.   I. Caswell, Jon.   II. Title.
HF5438.25.S23 1996   *95-50705*
658.85—dc20   *CIP*

Printing number

10 9 8 7 6 5 4 3 2 1

Contents

FOREWORD

The only thing that remains constant is change.

When people say something like this to you, what can you predict about them? Can you identify anything in this communication that will help you sell them on some product/service/idea? How do you package your communication with them? How do you package your product/service/idea for them? How do you motivate them?

There are clues in this phrase that let you know what they will do. You can know what to say in your presentation. You can know when and how to close. You can know how to package your communications. You can motivate them to want what you are selling. In short, you can sell more effectively than ever before. You only need to know how to decode this phrase.

Did you know that there are clues to improve your sales results from almost anything a prospect says? If you knew how to decode what they say to obtain these clues, you could dramatically improve your bottom-line. This book will help you understand how to predict and influence people based on the language they use. It is not difficult to learn, and you will be amazed at your results.

This may be the most powerful book about selling you will ever read. When you learn to *listen* to what people say, you know how to predict and influence their thinking and their behavior. When you can predict their thinking and their behavior, you can say and do the things that will influence them.

In this book, Marvin and Jon do a wonderful job of showing you how to listen and what to listen for. With the information you learn here, you will know how to recognize the patterns of any person you meet.

With *Selling the Way Your Customer Buys*, you are going to learn how to improve your results personally. When you learn and start to apply the information and techniques you find in this book, you will see dramatic improvement in your sales results. At the same time, you should also find a decrease in any work-related stress you might have. You will also find that your relationships with co-workers and with your management will improve.

This material is easy to learn, and with each chapter, you will have information and skills that you can immediately apply. When you have finished this book, you will have a system for improving your ability to predict and influence.

Take time and savor each of the skills. Practice each of these skills until they are automatic. After a short time, you will achieve a comfortable pace in the use of these skills, and you may even stop remembering which pattern a person is using, but you will automatically be responding in the way that gives you the most influence.

Good luck!

Rodger C. Bailey, President
International Screening Centers
Montevideo, Uruguay
and
Ft. Worth, Texas

Acknowledgments

The technology contained in this book is a foundation for understanding and predicting individual behavior. It is based on the clinical research of Leslie Cameron-Bandler, which initially identified the patterns. That, in turn, led Rodger Bailey to develop his "Language and Behavior Profile," which formulated the elicitation questions that are the basis of this book. His work was based on his studies of massive numbers of people in work situations.

We would like to thank Otilia Zmau for her patient and invaluable assistance in preparing the manuscript.

And speaking of those who are patient and invaluable, thanks especially to our wives, Annemarie and Linda.

1

The Secret to *All* Sales: Gaining *Deep* Rapport

You may have lost a big sale recently or you just want to sell more. Whatever the reason, the fact is you're reading a book about selling. If you'd never lost a sale, you might be relaxing someplace where a staff of butlers and maids took care of all your material comforts. Your chauffeur would have driven you to the bookstore where you would have bought any diverting book you wanted.

However, you're probably reading this book because you ring up more NO SALES than SALES. You can try to convince yourself that selling is a numbers game, but we all know there's more to it. Making a sale can be very personal because we make a connection when we succeed. You can sense when something happens between you and the client. Why aren't all sales calls that way?

We've all lost sales and when we did, which one of us didn't want to climb inside the customer's head to understand how they perceived the transaction? What better way than that to learn what we did wrong—or right? Did they dislike your visual presentation? Would they have thrived on simple phone contact, or did they expect you to come in, be chatty, ask about the kids? What convinced them to go with your competitor? What motivated them suddenly to decide after months of seeming to do nothing?

Selling the Way Your Customer Buys opens a door-way into your client's mind. With a few simple questions that you can easily weave into any conversation, you will learn to uncover your customers' unconscious mental blueprints: not the deep secrets of childhood, mind you, but the background patterns that keep them oriented and functioning in our complicated world. You will find an unconscious template with which they operate the computer we call the human brain.

At one level, the person across the desk is as pre-dictable as a laptop. And just as every computer has a disk operating system, or DOS, your customer has an operating system that functions in the background. This unconscious, background program we call *HOS* for *Human Operating System*.

This Human Operating System is composed of many elements and operates in every aspect of our lives. Each component is made up of patterns. These patterns drive our behavior. When you feel synchronized with someone, what we call *deep rapport* in this book, you have matched one or more of these unconscious patterns. Those patterns are strategies and concepts that drive our conscious feelings and actions. When we access these unconscious cues, people naturally feel comfortable with us and trust who we are and what we represent. In essence, rapport is having your behavior perfectly understood, accepted, and returned to you with an appropriate response. Rapport satisfies like no other human experience.

Unfortunately, the likelihood of your matching with someone else in more than one category is not very good. Researchers have identified more than fifty behav-ior categories (HOS components), and each category contains at least two patterns, often more, so the possible combinations quickly run into the millions. The odds of naturally matching every component of your customers' Human Operating System are astronomical. Please keep this in mind as you consider these odds: You're betting your paycheck. Sometimes only a single mismatch in one of these categories turns a sale sour. No wonder the average sales close is only one out of eight.

The problem is that most people haven't a clue about accessing these unconscious cues. If you asked a person outright what their cues were, they couldn't answer you even if they understood the question. But if you ask the right questions, questions designed to expose the patterns, and know what to listen for, they will present those strategies and concepts with surprising clarity. This book contains those questions and the key to deciphering the information they elicit.

We have simplified the identification of these patterns by clustering eight HOS components that relate to buying behavior. The table on the following page contains the questions that enable you to identify your customer's HOS Profile. As you can see, they are simple inquiries, easily worked into any conversation. However, don't be deceived by their seeming simplicity: They elicit powerful information that will make a big impact on your bottom line. To help you maintain the overall context of the HOS Profile, we have included this table of questions in each chapter, highlighting the question covered in that chapter (see page 4). Knowing your clients' HOS Profile improves your odds because you can quickly get into the zone of deep rapport by matching their unconscious strategies. You run no risk, you can even identify every one of those eight buying patterns over the phone.

We have observed the power of this knowledge countless times in real-time, real-world sales scenarios. Here is an example:

Michael, one of our clients, sells financial products. He had worked with a couple for three months trying to sell them a retirement program—a million-dollar transaction.

Category	Question
Motivating Language	For you, what is important about *selling?*
Motivating Direction	What do you want *from selling?* What will having *that* really do for you?
Motivating Source	How do you know *that you've done a good job?*
Process Approach	Why did you choose *to be a salesman/woman?*
Decision Strategy	How do you know that *your supplier/accountant/lawyer* is good *at their job?*
Convincer Strategy	How many times do they have to demonstrate this (*that they are good at their job*) before you are convinced?
Process Scope	Tell me about one of your favorite *working experiences.*
Process Relationship	What is the relationship between *what you are doing this year on your job and what you did last year on your job?*

The couple and Michael had a relationship that went back several years, and he felt they trusted him, especially since they had made the initial contact. But meeting after meeting he could not get them to commit. Finally he called us for advice. After a brief conversation, we suggested he change the structure of his presentation. Up to that point, he had made all the variables of the program equal and left the decision completely up to them. Not a bad strategy, but one that violated one of the couple's basic HOS components and kept them from trusting Michael. In the language of the HOS Profile, they sorted Externally (see Chapter 4). Without a concrete suggestion from the salesperson, whom they unconsciously viewed as the expert, they were lost. In their buying strategy program, a salesperson without a suggestion equaled a person who lacked commitment to the product. Instinctively they didn't want choices, they wanted guidance; that's why they had called Michael, a friend, instead of going through the Yellow Pages. But just as instinctively, Michael, who was Internal (see Chapter 4), thought they would want to decide for themselves, as he would have, rather than have him insert his opinion on such an important deal. What he viewed as an intrusion, they viewed as a necessary component of the transaction.

When Michael changed his presentation to indicate clearly which alternatives were best for the couple, they bought immediately.

Think of your client's brain as a computer that you are trying to access. You're sitting at the keyboard and you start typing on the keys. Nothing happens because you don't know what program he's running so you don't know which keys do what. To remedy that, you pull out the template from your own computer and put it on his keyboard and begin typing happily away. Again, nothing happens—NO SALE—because your customer's brain is running a different program, *his*. Your keyboard template doesn't match his, so you're pushing all the wrong buttons. Only by sheer luck or profound determination would you ever be able to decipher the commands necessary to operate his computer.

The HOS Profile allows you to tap into the buying program of every one of your customers. No longer will they seem mysterious. When you know their HOS Profiles, you will be able to give them information in the individual and unique ways in which they most readily accept it. You will create deep rapport with them because you will press the right keys for the outcome you want. Your closure rate will definitely increase. You'll have the time of your life with sales from customers who think you're one of the finest people they've ever met. And you are, because you're selling the way your customer buys.

IMPORTANT NOTE:
THE HOS PROFILE IS CONTEXT SPECIFIC.

Each of the following chapters revolves around a single question. The **BOLDFACE AND CAPITALIZED** portion represents the *formula* of the question and should not be changed. The *lower-case, italicized words* establish the *context* and can be changed to make them appropriate for your situation.

For example, here is the question from Chapter 2:

FOR YOU, WHAT IS IMPORTANT ABOUT

selling?
the product?
the service?
working?
relationships?
eating lunch?
going to church?

Each one of these particular endings, the *context* of the question, will elicit different responses because every person has different values in those contexts. The information you derive from the question *only applies within the context in which the question was asked.* You control that context according to how you frame the question. HOS information cannot be generalized between contexts. Thus, when adapting these questions to your repertoire of sales tools, change the contextual part of the question (*italics*) to fit your circumstances.

═══ 2 ═══

WORDS THAT MOTIVATE YOUR CUSTOMER

If you have ever visited a foreign country, you can easily recall the affinity you felt for people who could speak your language. Even in our own country, the groups we belong to are often defined by the specialized language we share: in our houses of worship, jobs, sports, and homes. All of us use words to which we have attached personal and unique meanngs. These words or phrases represent our values in a given context; these are the result of our individual experiences. The words themselves actually connect the person to the emotional experience, which, in turn, stimulates chemicals to flow in the brain, and this results in motivation. Without motivation, *nothing* happens: no rapport, no sale, no money!

So you can see how critical words can be, and that is why we call this category of the Human Operating System *Motivating Language*. These words reflect what we feel is important; they are as individual as fingerprints. When *these specific words* (and *not* their synonyms) are used, we respond with increased attention because we connect significance to them.

For a general example, let's use the context of baseball, which has a very specialized language.

Visualize a runner stealing second: He's speeding over the base path as fast as he can; the catcher springs

Category	Question
Motivating Language	For you, what is important about *selling?*
Motivating Direction	What do you want *from selling?* What will having *that* really do for you?
Motivating Source	How do you know *that you've done a good job?*
Process Approach	Why did you choose *to be a salesman/woman?*
Decision Strategy	How do you know that *your supplier/accountant/lawyer* is good *at their job?*
Convincer Strategy	How many times do they have to demonstrate this (*that they are good at their job*) before you are convinced?
Process Scope	Tell me about one of your favorite *working experiences.*
Process Relationship	What is the relationship between *what you are doing this year on your job and what you did last year on your job?*

from behind the plate; the pitcher jumps to one side as the ball sails straight over the mound; the second baseman moves into position, snags the throw and puts the tag on the runner as he slides into the bag! Safe or out? Everybody's attention locks on the umpire, who cocks his thumb over his shoulder and yells, "He's outta there!"

With one word—out—the umpire makes the offense unhappy and the defense ecstatic. Another way to say that is that he has destroyed rapport with the base runner and his team. By calling the runner out, he has met the defensive team's criteria for happiness, and by doing so has created rapport with them.

Using the right words and phrases goes a long way in creating rapport, the essential step in sales synergy. Unfortunately, those words and phrases are not so clear-cut in most sales situations as "safe" or "out."

Everywhere we interact with people, we create a special vocabulary that both generates and defines the relationships. Our special words keep strangers outside the gates and identify those we allow to pass. When you know the *Motivating Language* of another person, you have a key to that gate. In a selling situation, these power words represent your customer's *criteria for purchase*. When you meet those criteria, they will almost certainly buy.

These criteria words and phrases reflect our core belief systems, which is why the exact words are so powerful: they touch us at a deep level. Criteria words are power words. When we hear them, we naturally feel interested and predisposed to listening. If you want someone to feel drawn to what you have to offer, match *their* criteria words to *your* ideas and watch how quickly they take to heart what you have to say.

Few people realize the power of this kind of matching speech. Although very subtle, its impact is almost irresistible. When you use another person's words and phrases, you create rapport with them, and that is the essential step in sales synergy.

The Question for Motivating Language

Please answer this question on a sheet of paper or into a tape recorder.

FOR YOU, WHAT IS IMPORTANT ABOUT *selling?*

When you ask this question of a client, be sure to use the *formula* (**BOLDFACE CAPITALS**) and insert the appropriate *context (lower-case italics):* buying a car, a stereo, going to lunch, getting married, having a job, selling. It is important to qualify the question with "for you," otherwise you may get a general answer that will not give you the person's power words. You fill in the context.

How to Interpret What You Hear

The specific words contained in the answer are important. You must remember words exactly and use them in the same manner they were used. Synonyms or interpretations will not have the desired effect. When your client answers the question, pay attention to the emphasized words your prospect uses. These are power words. Feel free to ask the question for several contexts—a specific service or product, lunch, movies—any area where you would like to have influence. As we all know, having influence is a necessary precondition to making a sale, for if you cannot influence your client, how can your input sway their decision in your favor? If you are on the phone when you ask this question, jot down the exact answer. The criteria words will jump out at you. The following dialogue is a sample of how to get and use criteria words in a selling situation.

Fran:	I appreciate your time on the telephone this morning, Mr. James. Your assistant told me that you have been having problems with the copier system and might want to investigate other possibilities.
Mr. James:	I'm not interested in buying anything now, although I would like to find an inexpensive solution.
Fran:	There could be an inexpensive solution, and I would be happy to examine those possibilities. May I ask you a few questions before we get started?
Mr. James:	What would you like to ask?
Fran:	I'm curious, what is it that you want from your copying system? You know, FOR YOU, WHAT IS IMORTANT ABOUT *having a copying system?*
Mr. James:	Well, to make GOOD COPIES when we need them.
Fran:	What else?
Mr. James:	Well, I want a system that's DEPENDABLE AND MAKES GOOD, CLEAR COPIES. We need clear copies because we have to use them in multiple presentations.

Fran:	So you want A DEPENDABLE SYSTEM that makes GOOD, CLEAR COPIES. What else is really important to you?
Mr. James:	I want a system that's EASY TO USE. I'm tired of training new people on the machine or answering questions about how it works. I'm too busy to stop every ten minutes to help with the copier. You know, there is one thing I wish our system had, I want it to COPY BOTH SIDES WITHOUT HAVING TO MANUALLY RE-FEED THE PAPER. Is there a machine that will do that and is NOT VERY EXPENSIVE?
Fran:	Oh yes, there are a number of ways to go that are NOT VERY EXPENSIVE. By the way, what kind of budget are you working with?
Mr. James:	I have to STAY UNDER $800, and I have to GET A GOOD TRADE-IN on the equipment I'm using now.

At this point, Fran has succeeded in getting Mr. James's criteria for purchasing a new copier. The words are simple to pick out of conversation. Just as we have emphasized the words here, people emphasize their criteria words when speaking by changing their tonality.

Fran has already used Mr. James's criteria words, and to maximize her effectiveness she must use them throughout her presentation and close. When Mr. James believes that these criteria—NOT VERY EXPENSIVE, DEPENDABLE, EASY TO USE, GOOD CLEAR COPIES,

COPY BOTH SIDES WITHOUT HAVING TO MANU-
ALLY RE-FEED THE PAPER, UNDER $800, and A
GOOD TRADE-IN—are met, he will purchase a copier.
By using his exact words in relation to her own product,
Fran matches her copiers to the criteria that motivate Mr.
James to buy. Here is an example of how she can do that.

> *Fran:*   Mr. James, I want to put together a
> few possible solutions for you that
> are NOT VERY EXPENSIVE and will
> give you equipment that makes
> GOOD, CLEAR COPIES and is very
> DEPENDABLE. I will also make sure
> that it is EASY TO USE. I'm sure that I
> can supply a machine that COPIES
> ON BOTH SIDES WITHOUT HAV-
> ING TO RE-FEED THE PAPER
> MANUALLY. It will take me two
> days to gather the information for
> you, so would a meeting on Thursday
> morning fit your schedule, sometime
> before lunch?

How Motivating Language Affects the Sales Cycle

As we said earlier, in a sales situation, your prospect's
Motivating Language represents his or her criteria for
purchase. Only when you and your product meet those
standards will you make the sale.

Your clients will feel you understand their needs
when you respond to them using their own words. You
will build a positive atmosphere of friendly trust, and
that will put them in the mood to hear what you have to
say.

This simple question—**FOR YOU, WHAT IS IMPORTANT ABOUT** (*your product or service*)—gives you invaluable information about how to align yourself and your product. Work the question into the first part of your initial conversation so you can use your prospect's criteria words throughout the transaction. Use them to increase the odds of your pitch being heard favorably.

If someone has a long list of criteria, it could be time for a reality check: Can you actually satisfy this person? More than six or seven items may indicate an unrealistic customer. It could mean it's time to let the competition win one.

On the other hand, if your client answers with only one very general word, it could indicate that he or she really doesn't know what is wanted. If the person responds with the criterion that it will make them HAPPY, that doesn't tell you much. You need to find out the specifics of what HAPPY looks, sounds, or feels like to them. How will the person recognize when he or she is HAPPY? Despite the generality of HAPPY, it does represent the client's values in this context. We, as the service provider, must use the word *happy*. At the same time, we must understand what the customer means by that word so we can give the client what he or she wants.

Points to Remember:
Too many criteria words may mean a prospect can't be satisfied.

Too few criteria words may mean the prospect hasn't delineated his or her needs. Find out what the customer means specifically.

Success Equals Learning to Listen

The best way to become comfortable gleaning Motivating Language from conversation is to spend several days asking only this question from the HOS Profile. Ask it of anybody you meet, and ask it with a variety of contexts. The point here is to get used to hearing responses and identifying the words.

Once you get a person's criteria words, use them in your conversation and carefully observe the response. Typically, people exhibit an increased interest in what you are saying. They will do this by staying in rapport with you, which means asking you questions, following your examples without interruption, continuing to engage you in conversation, or just generally showing interest.

Alternative Questions

It may seem awkward to you to ask the question in exactly the formula we have given it. If so, here is an alternative formula that will elicit your client's power words.

WHAT DO YOU REALLY WANT IN AN *investment?*

> *car?*
> *stereo?*
> *job?*
> *computer?*

What Is Your Motivating Language

If you answered the question at the beginning of the chapter—FOR YOU, WHAT IS IMPORTANT ABOUT SELLING, you now know your hot-button words for the context of selling. In other words, for you to be happy in your sales situation, you must feel that those criteria are being met. When other people use these words, it will get your attention. Please copy them to the Motivating Language box of the HOS Profile Chart on pages 163–164.

Practice Makes Perfect

The idea behind Motivating Language is quite simple: Each of us has words and phrases that mean something unique to us and to which we respond with increased attention. These hot-button words change with context, just as you have different criteria for a car, a tennis partner, or a college for your kids.

Gaining access to another person's criteria is as easy as asking the question **FOR YOU, WHAT IS IMPORTANT ABOUT** _____? See if you can pick out the customer's Motivating Language in the following examples. Answers appear on pages 18–19.

Example 1

> *Mork:*   What do you really want in a relationship?
>
> *Mindy:*   Well, I guess I want to know that we are friends and can depend on each other in a tough situation. You know, a person that respects you and listens to you when you need to talk. It would be great also if they liked the outdoors and hiking.

Example 2

> *Tory:*   You know, I just don't feel like eating out.

Megan:	Well, what's important about eating out?
Tory:	You mean, in general? It's really good for the economy, I know that.
Megan:	No, no, I mean, what's important about it *to you?*
Tory:	Well, you know, the regular stuff—exotic food, good selection of imported beers, no loud music, uhhh, no cockroaches, and cute waitresses that pay a lot of attention to me. You know what, I don't want to have to drive 30 miles to eat either: It needs to be pretty close by.
Megan:	How close is "pretty close"?
Tory:	Ten, eleven miles, fifteen max.

Example 3

Gifford:	For you, what is really important about how accounts receivable should function?
Robbins:	We need to get paid faster and reduce nonpayments. I am tired of supplying distributors who are slow-pay and then go out of business. Those guys live on my credit and don't even pay for it.

Example 4

Shelby:	For you, what is really important about the investments you buy?

Linda: I want something that has long-term potential and can give me a good return with no risk to my initial investment. I want security in the future and a lump sum to live on when I'm older.

Reviewing further is essential to your learning how to distinguish Motivating Language from the torment of words that come pouring out when you ask people what's important to them. We suggest that you ask this question in a variety of contexts to anyone who will let you record their answer on tape. At home, play their answers until you can identify their hot-button words and phrases. They will emphasize their answers with intonations just as we have emphasized the answers to these review examples.

Answers to Review

Example 1

Mindy: Well, I guess I want to know that we are FRIENDS and can DEPEND ON EACH OTHER in a tough situation. You know, a person that RESPECTS you and LISTENS to you when you need to talk. It would be great also if they LIKED THE OUTDOORS AND HIKING.

Example 2

Notice the result of Megan's failure to contextualize the question with "for you": She had to repeat the question with the proper context to get the information she wanted.

Tory:	Well, you know, the regular stuff— EXOTIC FOOD, good selection of IMPORTED BEERS, NO LOUD MUSIC, uhhh, NO COCKROACHES, and CUTE WAITRESSES that pay a lot of attention to me. You know what, I don't want to have to drive 30 miles to eat either: It needs to be PRETTY CLOSE BY.

Example 3

Robbins:	We need to GET PAID FASTER and REDUCE NONPAYMENTS. I am tired of supplying distributors who are slow-pay and then go out of business. Those guys live on my credit and don't even pay for it.

Example 4

Linda:	I want something that has LONG-TERM POTENTIAL and can give me A GOOD RETURN with NO RISK TO MY INITIAL INVESTMENT. I want SECURITY IN THE FUTURE and a LUMP SUM TO LIVE ON WHEN I'M OLDER.

=== 3 ===

ENTHUSIASM *CAN* KILL THE SALE

You probably have a lot of enthusiasm for what you sell. After all the sales training and pump-you-up weekends you've participated in, you'd better be enthusiastic, right? If you didn't have a big reserve of positive energy, you'd never get through all the negativity and rudeness that you run into in the sales jungle.

No doubt all that installed bravado has served you well personally, but it may have turned off your clients. Not all of them, mind you, but some. There are people out there, and you have undoubtedly run into them, who possess the intuitive belief that enthusiastic people are not to be trusted. On the other hand, there are people who intuitively believe that you can't trust anyone who isn't enthusiastic. The trick is knowing which is which and dealing with each in the way that makes them feel comfortable.

Motivating Direction

For our purposes, people who appreciate enthusiasm are goal-motivated: They set an objective and work *toward* attaining it. At the other end of the spectrum are those who detest goals: These people see problems and instinctively work to get *away from* them. Because of the directional nature of the two patterns involved, we call this category of the HOS Profile "Motivating Direction."

Category	Question
Motivating Language	For you, what is important about *selling?*
Motivating Direction	What do you want *from selling?* What will having *that* really do for you?
Motivating Source	How do you know *that you've done a good job?*
Process Approach	Why did you choose *to be a salesman/woman?*
Decision Strategy	How do you know that *your supplier/accountant/lawyer* is good *at their job?*
Convincer Strategy	How many times do they have to demonstrate this (*that they are good at their job*) before you are convinced?
Process Scope	Tell me about one of your favorite *working experiences.*
Process Relationship	What is the relationship between *what you are doing this year on your job and what you did last year on your job?*

The Toward Pattern

The buzzword of Toward behavior is *goals*. People who display this type of behavior understand *goals* and are motivated by them. In fact, goals motivate them to the point that they often ignore difficulties and are certain to discount negative consequences. Toward people just don't give any energy to problems: It's the goal that matters, what gets them up in the morning and out into the day. They want to gain; they want to attain and achieve.

The Away-From Pattern

The key word for the Away-From person is *avoid*. People with this pattern see *problems*, in fact, this is their great benefit. This is especially true in an organization with a lot of Toward people who refuse to acknowledge what can go wrong. Away-From individuals are motivated to avoid the problems they recognize. Just as problems disorient the Toward person, goals trip up Away-From people. They have difficulty articulating objectives and feel confused when given goals to accomplish. Rather than seeing the benefits goal achievement will bring, they only see the problems that can arise in working toward them. Because they search out what can go wrong, Away-From people are valuable on a team. However, they may be labeled as party poopers and killjoys by those whom they often see as risk-takers. The Toward person will very likely think of the Away-From personality as negative.

People Can Be In-between

Motivating Direction is a continuum. In other words, people can combine the Toward and Away-From patterns to different degrees. In addition, there are those who exhibit both patterns equally: Those people are motivated by goals *and* they can identify what can go wrong. As you listen to a variety of people answer this question, you will naturally learn to distinguish the degree to which each pattern expresses in those who are not wholly Toward or Away-From.

The Question for Motivating Direction

The following questions reveal your Motivating Direction for the context of selling. (Remember, the **BOLD-FACED AND CAPITALIZED** part of the question is the formula; the *lower-case, italicized* portion is the context, which is the part you would modify by filling in your product or service.) Please answer these two questions for yourself on a sheet of paper or into a tape recorder.

1. **WHAT DO YOU WANT** *from selling*?
2. **WHAT WILL HAVING** *that* **REALLY DO FOR YOU?**

The answer to the first question will consist of criteria words, typically the same ones (depending on the context you set) elicited by the Motivating Language question. It is important to remember those words and phrases because you ask the second question by inserting them into the formula. For example, if you answered the first question—What do you want from selling— with "more money," the second question would be phrased, "What will having *more money* do for you?" The information that tells you whether someone is Toward or Away-From comes from the second question. If you don't get a clear reading of your client's motivational compass, keep asking the question, inserting the last answer you got, until you feel you are clear on what having those things will do for the person: Will it *add* to their life in some way or will it *help them avoid* something? Are they attracted or repelled?

How to Interpret What You Hear

We lace our conversation with our Motivating Direction. Toward people answer the question with things they hope to achieve or gain. If you ask them what having a good job will do for them, they will say things like "It will pay for a new car" or "I can meet new people that are more like me" or "It will buy me the time to spend with my family." A Toward person talks about how *attaining* goals will *benefit* life. These people can label what their goals will *give* them. An Away-From person won't do that.

Away-From speech contains things to be avoided. In answering the question regarding a job, they will say things like "It keeps me from getting evicted" or "It gives me security" or "It keeps me off the streets." A person who uses the phrase "keep from" is almost certainly Away-From.

Here is what Mr. James, the man who was looking for an inexpensive copier, might sound like as an Away-From:

Fran:	Mr. James, **WHAT WILL HAVING** a copying system that is dependable, makes good clear copies, is easy to use, and is not expensive **REALLY DO FOR YOU?** [Notice that Fran has inserted Mr. James's criteria words into the formula.]
Mr. James:	What do you mean, what will it do for me?

Fran:	You know, what will it really ... do for ... *you?*
Mr. James:	Well, I guess it will *keep me from losing time and being so frustrated* when I need copies and can't finish a project.

Clearly, Mr. James has identified a problem in his copier situation: It's costing him time and frustration. But notice also that he doesn't really understand the question because he asks for clarification. An Away-From doesn't conceive of the world as doing anything for him. To sell Mr. James, Fran will have to help him avoid his problem, either by solving it or by helping him dodge it.

Now let's listen to the speech pattern of a Toward Mr. James as he answers the same question:

Mr. James:	Well, I guess I'll be able to *accomplish a lot more work and take on some other projects.*

Clearly, Mr. James is thinking about how a new copier will enhance his position. He is not aiming to avoid unpleasant consequences.

Let's look at an Away-From pattern in another context.

Alan:	Steve, you talked about wanting to have an investment that is *safe* and still gives you a *return that would stay ahead of inflation.* **WHAT WOULD HAVING** *that kind of investment* **REALLY DO FOR YOU?**
Steve:	Well, if you could find something like that, I could relax, knowing that my

savings would not lose their buying power when I retired.

Obviously, Steve is an Away-From investor. He wants to be sure he keeps his savings from losing their value. He indicates no interest in maximizing his return or seeking out high yields. He wants to *avoid* losing money.

Here's how a Toward investor would answer the same question:

> **Sarah:**   It will give me an opportunity to grow my excess cash flow into something that will let me travel and really enjoy my retirement.

Sarah's answer is completely different. She talks about opportunity and growth and identifies options that are exciting to her. Travel and enjoyment certainly add to her life; they are not something she is trying to avoid. She doesn't entertain any of the worry we heard in Steve's answer: Sarah simply isn't focused on what can go wrong.

How Motivating Direction Affects the Sales Cycle

As you can imagine, a mismatch in Motivating Direction can create a lot of problems for a salesperson. A goal-motivated salesman will get nowhere with a client who only sees what can go wrong getting there. It is unlikely that he or she will build the rapport necessary to consummate a deal. The Away-From buyer will continually pick apart the gains and benefits the Toward salesman identifies. Have you ever had a customer like that?

Or consider the Away-From saleswoman who insists on pointing out the client's current problems to show how the product solves them. Unfortunately, the Toward client needs to hear how he or she benefits from the purchase. To be motivated to buy, he or she must be convinced that something is to be gained. Avoiding problems does not motivate this prospect.

Matching your clients' Motivating Direction is a very important step in building rapport: If you are not going in the same direction, you will not get to the checkbook at the same time. When you match their picture of the world, they sense that you innately understand. They will trust you. Failing to match in this category creates an uneasy feeling that you are out of sync with your customer.

Let's take a look at how Alan handled his Toward and Away-From customers.

Toward Customer

> *Alan:*   Sarah, when your money is invested you can begin examining even more possibilities of how to spend your retirement years. You can even begin doing those things right now.

Alan knows that Sarah needs something to aim for, something that she believes will improve her retirement. By relating that future goal to the current moment, he enlivens the goal in a way that is more compelling than leaving it in some vague future.

Alan's approach with the Away-From Steve has to be different. Here's how he phrases his response:

Away-From Customer

> *Alan:*   When your money is safely invested in this program you can rest easy knowing

that you won't be losing your equity to inflation.

When closing Away-From buyers, it is crucial to reassure them that they will avoid the problems they have identified for you. Since they want to be "kept from" those difficulties, it's important to tell them that the problem "won't be" a problem if they use your product or service. The form of the communication is

---

"I want to keep from having this happen"

to which you answer

"You won't have that problem if you give us the business."

You cannot dismiss the problem and concentrate on what they may attain, gain, or achieve because that does nothing to ease their instinct that something can go wrong.

To master this part of the HOS Profile, do the review that follows and then spend several days asking only these two questions of as many people as possible.

WHAT DO YOU WANT FROM _____?
WHAT WILL HAVING *that* **DO FOR YOU?**

Listen closely to the answers and before long you will be able to identify each pattern easily and consistently. Practice matching each speech pattern and observe the effects on rapport when you match or mismatch. At first you may feel awkward outside your own pattern, but that will change as you see how quickly people respond to your matching speech.

What is Your Motivating Direction?

Now evaluate your own answers to the questions "What do you want from selling?" and "What will having that do for you?" Are you a goal-oriented Toward achiever, or are you a problem-spotting Away-From avoider? Do you want to attain and gain, or do you want to steer clear and get rid of? If you can't quite decide, keep asking yourself the second question: What will having that (the criteria you used to answer the first question) do for me?

When you are clear about your pattern, mark the appropriate box in the HOS Profile on pages 163–164.

Practice Makes Perfect

The patterns of the Motivating Direction category are easy to spot: Does the person answer with benefits or problems? Pick out the patterns in these examples. Answers appear on pages 31–33.

Example 1

Myrna: What will having a relationship like the one you want really do for you?

Karla: It will keep me from having to worry about having someone to grow old with.

Example 2

Bryan: What will having the kind of investment you want really do for you?

Linda: I will be able to plan for the future and reach my goals.

Example 3

Peter: What will having the kind of invest-
            ment you want really do for you?

Paul: I can get old without worrying, and I
            can have the cash to have some fun.

Example 4

Lisa: What will having the kind of class you
            want really do for you?

Paul: That's easy. It would keep me up on all
            the recent developments in optics so I
            could stay on my career track and keep
            the bill collectors away from my door.

Reviewing further is essential to learning how to distinguish the patterns in Motivating Direction. We suggest that you ask this question, in a variety of contexts, of anyone who will let you record their answer on tape. At home, play their answers until you are sure whether they are giving you a benefit, a problem, or a combination of the two. Do they relate to goals or to what can go wrong? Where is their focus?

Answers to the Review

Example 1

Myrna: What will having a relationship like the
            one you want really do for you?

Karla: It will KEEP ME FROM HAVING TO
            WORRY about having someone to grow
            old with.

Karla is AWAY FROM in relationships: She wants to avoid worrying.

Example 2

> *Bryan:*   What will having the kind of invest-
>   ment you want really do for you?

> *Linda:*   I will be able to PLAN FOR THE
>   FUTURE AND REACH MY GOALS.

Linda is a TOWARD investor: She understands goals.

Example 3

> *Peter:*   What will having the kind of invest-
>   ment you want really do for you?

> *Paul:*   I can get old WITHOUT WORRYING,
>   and I can HAVE THE CASH TO HAVE
>   SOME FUN.

Paul is a mxed-pattern investor, what we call EQUALLY TOWARD & AWAY FROM: He wants to avoid worrying, and he wants to have fun.

Example 4

> *Lisa:*   What will having the kind of class you
>   want really do for you?

> *Eric:*   That's easy, it would KEEP ME UP ON
>   all the recent developments in optics so
>   I could STAY ON MY CAREER TRACK
>   and KEEP THE BILL COLLECTORS
>   AWAY from my door.

Eric is also a mixed pattern, what we call MORE TOWARD THAN AWAY FROM: He answers with two TOWARD patterns and one AWAY FROM. He understands goals ("career track"), and he sees how a class could benefit him ("keep me up on"), but he also wants to avoid those bill collectors. In responding to him, focus on TOWARD languages and speech patterns, but be sure to address any problems he identifies.

4

WHO *REALLY* TELLS YOUR CUSTOMER TO SAY YES?

Do you have a friend or know someone who is really hard-headed and refuses to take input from you or anyone else? It's as if no opinion but their own has any validity.

It's also likely that you've come across that person's opposite, the man or woman who seems to have no opinion of his or her own and will follow your lead, wherever it goes.

Motivating Source

These two patterns represent the poles on a continuum of behavior that makes up a basic part of the HOS Profile: the source of a person's motivation. Are they motivated by circumstances outside themselves or within? Motivating Source reaches far into our behavior. This part of the Human Operating System measures whether a person values input from others or makes decisions independently. We have labeled the patterns that make it up as External and Internal.

Recently a client called Marvin asking him to accompany a key salesperson on a major presentation. The client explained that this one order was worth several mil-

Category	*Question*
Motivating Language	For you, what is important about *selling?*
Motivating Direction	What do you want *from selling?* What will having *that* really do for you?
Motivating Source	How do you know *that you've done a good job?*
Process Approach	Why did you choose *to be a salesman/woman?*
Decision Strategy	How do you know that *your supplier/accountant/lawyer* is good *at their job?*
Convincer Strategy	How many times do they have to demonstrate this (*that they are good at their job*) before you are convinced?
Process Scope	Tell me about one of your favorite *working experiences.*
Process Relationship	What is the relationship between *what you are doing this year on your job and what you did last year on your job?*

lion dollars to the company, and the company wanted him to observe the meeting and provide feedback to the sales executive and the organization. He was introduced as part of a re-engineering team that was evaluating manufacturing processes and human applications, and he sat inconspicuously to the customer's right and off to the side.

The salesman launched into his presentation, and Marvin immediately noticed that he continually referred to himself and his decision about how good the product was and how it fit very well into the customer's needs. Several times he either said or implied how important he felt it was that the customer do exactly what the salesman wanted, which basically was to buy the product. Every time the sales executive talked about what he thought, Marvin observed that the customer's facial muscles tightened, which is a clear indication that the man was not aligned with the salesman's language.

To Marvin this indicated that the customer was Internal and did not want to be given directions. Intuitively, the sales executive felt his client's attention slipping away and instinctively pressed harder. Finally, in frustration the customer turned to Marvin and said, "Well, you're the re-engineering expert, what do you think about what Bill is saying about how your products could fit into our future growth plans?"

Of course, Marvin knew next to nothing about the technology that was being pitched, but he did understand that the sales executive had lost rapport with the client. If the sale was to be salvaged, he would have to re-establish goodwill, so he said that the information that had already been presented was only information that he, the customer, could examine and determine whether it was appropriate for the future growth of the company. "You're the only person who can make that decision, so whatever I say will just be added information," Marvin concluded.

Immediately, he noticed the customer's cheek muscles relax, and he smiled as he said, "You know, that's exactly right. I am the only person that could make that decision." As the conversation continued, the man turned his chair toward Marvin and began talking to him instead of the salesman. After a few minutes, he stood up and asked if Marvin would like to go to the cafeteria, have a cup of coffee, and talk in a more relaxed environment while the sales executive met with the engineering manager to work out the specifics of the product integration. Marvin and the president had a great cup of coffee, a good conversation, and the sale was made.

This story points out how important it is to determine whether an individual's Motivating Source is Internal or External. In this case, the president of the company sorted Internally, which meant that he was the person who could make the decision. It also meant that he would subconsciously resist anyone telling him what he should do. The merest suggestion that someone else's input is required breaks rapport with an Internal. The president aligned with Marvin because he presented a language pattern that aligned with the way the man's brain sorted for Motivating Source. When Marvin said that "only he could make that decision," he felt instinctively that Marvin understood him.

It's a complex world out there: Some people won't ever do what you tell them to do, and others won't do anything unless you tell them to. The trick is knowing how to tell one from the other, and you're about to find out exactly how that's done.

The External Pattern

A person with the External pattern relies on the evaluations and judgments of other people to know whether he has done a good job. In forming opinions, Externals depend on criteria and judgments outside themselves. They readily conform to other people's beliefs and measure themselves by the criteria of others, particularly those of their supervisors, customers, and friends.

In a sales situation, they depend on what others decide. What motivates them to make a decision comes from what other people say.

The Internal Pattern

Persons with the Internal pattern do not accept direction from other people. In forming their opinions, they will take outside input and evaluate it against their personal value systems. They are perfectly capable and willing to evaluate their own performance by their own standards, no matter where they are in the corporate hierarchy. Criteria set by another person is irrelevant when evaluating their own performance. In the world of the Internal, only their own opinion really matters.

Internal and External represent the two poles of a continuum of behavior. As with any continuum, few people are going to be completely Internal or External, but one or the other pattern will predominate in a given context. Your clients will continually use speech patterns that demonstrate whether they rely on their own criteria or the judgments of others in making decisions. This feature of the HOS program determines the influencing language that will be most effective. With the Internal you will acknowledge that it is a decision they have to make on their own and do your best not to insert your opinion into the process. On the other hand, with Externals you can freely give input because they will feel lost without it.

The Question for Motivating Source

Your answer to the following question reveals your Motivating Source. Please answer it for yourself on a sheet of paper or into a tape recorder.

HOW DO YOU KNOW *that you've done a good job?*

The answer to this question demonstrates the source of your motivation in the context of your job. Do you need input from others or are your opinions sufficient? In the next section, you will learn how to spot the speech patterns that indicate Internal and External Motivating Source.

How to Interpret What You Hear

Dialogue A

Joan
(salesperson):   Jim, we've talked about the kinds of investments you want and what they will really do for you. I am wondering, in the past when you made decisions about investing, **HOW DID YOU KNOW THAT YOU MADE A GOOD DECISION** at the time you made it?

Jim: I guess I just kind of felt it inside. You know, Joan, when you make a decision you just know when it's right.

Dialogue B

Joan: Terry, we've talked about the kinds of investments you want and what they will really do for you. I am wondering, in the past when you made decisions about investing, **HOW DID YOU KNOW THAT YOU MADE A GOOD DECISION** at the time you made it?

Terry: I listened to the feedback of my accountant and my two partners. If they said it looked like a good deal, well, with that kind of endorsement, I just felt I had to take the risk. And was I glad I did. It turned out to be a great investment.

What do you notice in the answers of Joan's two prospects? Jim and Terry have very different responses to her question.

Jim responds in typical Internal fashion: He just knows. Internals will use phrases like "I know" and "personal satisfaction." They will often have a list of criteria that constitutes the measure of how they know something is good: "I know it's good because. . . ."

Terry uses feedback to decide. He solicits and listens to the opinions of others before he acts. The content of an External's answer to this question refers to other people or the criteria of other people. There is no emphasis on personal satisfaction or some hazy, almost mystical "I just know": They know because someone tells them. More than any speech pattern or particular language, content is the evidence of an External code in the HOS program: Are other people or their criteria involved in the answer?

How the Motivating Source Affects the Sales Cycle

A person's Motivating Source dictates the kind of close you will use. For instance, do you think testimonials are effective with Internal customers? They couldn't care less what someone else thinks about your product. They will make up their minds without benefit of your opinion, thank you very much. On the other hand, an External will relish what others have to say.

This is how Joan responded to Jim, the Internal prospect:

> *Joan:*   I understand what you're saying, Jim. Well, we've talked about the Ajax fund and how it meets your particular needs. You have all the data and have examined it and ONLY YOU CAN MAKE THE DECISION to get in the program today. HOW DO YOU WANT TO HANDLE THIS?

Notice how Joan leaves the decision completely with Jim. Now observe how she changes this close when she talks to Terry, the External:

> *Joan:*   I understand what you're saying, Terry. We've talked about the Ajax fund and how it meets your particular needs. Many of my clients who have wanted similar returns and stability have been very happy in the fund. You have all the data and have examined it, and based on what you have told me, Terry, THIS IS THE FOUNDATION INVESTMENT FUND FOR YOU. Let's finish this receipt form SO YOU CAN JOIN A GROUP OF SATISFIED CLIENTS.

With Terry, Joan inserts herself more clearly into the process, externalizing the criteria and guiding by his decision. She also stresses the satisfaction of others involved in the program, something that would be completely wasted on Jim or any Internal.

You will certainly encounter people who mix Internal and External language patterns. When they answer the question, note the first pattern they use and emphasize that one in your presentation. Follow up with the other pattern. If they mix patterns, mix your language appropriately.

We have found that people sometimes interpret Motivating Source prematurely. Here is an example of misreading the Motivating Source. A participant in one of our seminars related this story. She had evaluated one of her clients, a CEO, as an External because he had to get his operating officer's feedback before making a decision. Despite her evaluation, she could not influence him by using External response language. She did manage to get a second meeting, attended by the operating officer, and she saw that her judgment had been premature. The CEO did ask for the man's opinion, but he clearly evaluated his response against his own criteria. He made decisions internally. With that information, she changed her language to that of Internal, removing herself and her criteria from the table, and closed the sale. "I sold the engagement because I changed my language pattern to match his Motivating Source," she said. "I gave the whole decision over to him, and he decided." That's what Internals do best.

We suggest that you spend several days just asking this one question of as many people as you can. With only a little practice, you will quickly develop the ability to hear and evaluate the clues to a person's Motivating Source. After you have deciphered that pattern, match it by giving them the appropriate cues. Then, intentionally mismatch and observe any changes in the quality of the interaction.

Alternative Questions

HOW DO YOU KNOW *that you've made a good decision at the time you made it?*
HOW DO YOU KNOW *you've seen a good movie?*
HOW DO YOU KNOW *a restaurant is good?*

What Is Your Motivating Source?

How did you answer the question "How do you know that you've done a good job?" Did your answer have the mysterious "I just know" pattern, or do you rely on outside input to make decisions? Please mark your pattern in the appropriate box of the HOS Profile Chart on pages 163–164.

Practice Makes Perfect

The Internal/External patterns of the Motivating Source category are easy to spot: Does the person make the decision within themselves or do they allow other people to have input? Answers appear on pages 45–47.

Example 1

> *Myrna:* How did you know that you made a good decision on the last car you bought, at the time you bought it?

> *Karla:* I felt it the moment I sat in the driver's seat, it was definitely right for me.

Example 2

> *Bryan:* How did you know that you made a good decision on the last car you bought, at the time you bought it?

> *Linda:* After all the research and driving around I had to go with what the salesman was telling me. He's in the business, after all, and should know what he's talking about.

Example 3

> *Peter:* How did you know you did a good job on that last project?

> *Paul:* Well, everyone I talked to told me what a great job I did. Plus I felt good about the way things happened.

Example 4

> *Lisa:* How did you know you did a good job on that last project?

> *Laura:* I just knew it. It seemed to me the results were obvious.

Reviewing further is essential to learning how to distinguish the patterns in Motivating Source. We suggest that you ask this question, in a variety of contexts, of anyone who will let you record their answer on tape. At home, play their answers until you are sure whether they make decisions internally or need input from other people.

Answers to the Review

Example 1

> *Myrna:* How did you know that you made a good decision on the last car you bought, at the time you bought it?

> *Karla:*   I FELT IT the moment I sat in the driver's
>   seat, it was definitely RIGHT FOR ME.

Karla is an Internal: She knew when *her* criteria were met.

Example 2

> *Bryan:*   How did you know that you made a
>   good decision on the last car you bought,
>   at the time you bought it?
>
> *Linda:*   After all the research and driving around
>   I HAD TO GO WITH WHAT THE
>   SALESMAN WAS TELLING ME. He's in
>   the business, after all, and should know
>   what he's talking about.

Linda is an External: She values the salesman's opinion
over her own.

Example 3

> *Peter:*   How did you know you did a good job
>   on that last project?
>
> *Paul:*   Well, EVERYONE I TALKED TO TOLD ME
>   WHAT A GREAT JOB I DID. Plus I FELT
>   GOOD about the way things had happened.

Paul is a mixed pattern, equally Internal and External:
He takes into account the opinions of others, but he also
knows within himself.

Example 4

> *Lisa:*   How did you know you did a good job
>   on that last project?

> **Laura:** I JUST KNEW IT. IT SEEMED TO ME, the results were obvious.

Laura is Internal: I, me, and nobody else.

Review of Chapters 2, 3, & 4

This three-chapter review is an opportunity for you to practice evaluating speech patterns. We will eavesdrop on the conversation of Tim Huggins, a business consultant, and Riley Miller, the CEO of a small manufacturing company. Huggins wants to use the HOS information to help him get a consulting contract. Every few chapters throughout the book, we will drop in on their conversation. In this installment, the two men have just met after they were networked together by a mutual friend. This conversation will serve as the foundation for Huggins's knowledge of what the customer wants and how best to serve him. Your assignment is to pick out Miller's Motivating Language, and his HOS patterns for Motivating Direction and Motivating Source: Is he Toward or Away-From? Is he Internal or External? What are his hot-button words?

> **Miller:** Good morning. Come in my office and let's find out why Bill thought we should meet.
>
> **Huggins:** I appreciate your time and I'm anxious to learn more about your company.
>
> **Miller:** I really don't have much time this morning. I have another meeting in 30 minutes.

Huggins: Sounds like you're pretty busy. Bill said that you needed some consulting work, so I'm wondering, what kind of consulting work you really want?

Miller: Well, the truth is, I'm having a helluva delay in my accounts receivable, and I'm suspicious that we're not handling that function very well. I'm sure there's room for improvement.

Huggins: Regarding your accounts receivable, for you, what is important about how it should function?

Miller: We have to get paid faster and reduce non-payments. I'm tired of supplying distributors who are slow-pay and then go out of business. These guys are living on my credit and not even paying for it.

Huggins: I've had the opportunity to help a number of manufacturers with similar needs. In this area of our business, we have developed functions that identify distributors that are potentially slow-pay and are not financially sound. Those are the ones that usually go out of business after they receive your products. The functions we have developed also help get money in faster.

Miller: That sounds very interesting. What would it cost for us to use you?

Huggins: That depends on a number of things. For instance, I would need to know how your functions are organized now. I would need to evaluate the systems you have that support those functions, and I would have to hear more about the results you want to achieve. If you had the kind of accounts receivable function that gave you the things you wanted, what would that really do for you or your company?

Miller: Well, it would keep me from losing money and wasting time with dead-beats. The only way we can grow is to have cash flow moving and spending time getting more and better customers. Without that we aren't going to be around for my kids to benefit.

Huggins: I can appreciate what you're saying, it's the same in my business: If we don't have the supporting business functions to protect us from fast-talking deadbeats, we can't get better, and we can sure lose what we've been working for. That's not the lesson we want to teach our kids.

Miller: You've got that right. How long would it take for you to examine our present functions and tell me what you can do and give me an estimate of what it will cost?

Huggins: If I could spend a full day with your accounts receivable people and some more time with you, I will have enough information to prepare a bid that outlines my services and the cost. Have you ever used a consulting service before?

Miller: Yes, once when we were setting up an assembly facility.

Huggins: I'm curious, when you hired the consultants, how did you know that you hired the right group?

Miller: I don't think I've ever been asked that before. It's a good question. I listened to their pitches and I checked their references. After I examined all the inputs, I had a clear sense of who would do the best job.

Huggins: I'm impressed that you are so thorough when making these kinds of decisions. You definitely don't want to make a mistake when it comes to your accounts receivable. I will certainly supply you with names and phone numbers of past clients so you can confirm my competence. They can tell you the results of my services. I'll be happy to supply you with any other information you might need, but I recognize that only you can make this decision.

Miller: I want you to know that I am evaluating another organization, and I will be comparing your proposal to theirs.

Huggins:	It's good that you're making compar- isons. I would be able to schedule time next week to spend here. What would be the best time for you so that we can get the information I need to develop a proposal?
Miller:	The middle of the week, but I need to check with my accounts receiv- able manager first and then confirm a time.
Huggins:	Great, I know that time is impor- tant, so once my information gather- ing is complete, I will be able to help you get paid faster and identify those deadbeats before you waste your time or money. I notice that we're getting close to your next appointment.
Miller:	That's true. Call me this afternoon to set up a schedule for next week.
Huggins:	Good. Thanks for your time and I'll call this afternoon.

Answers to the Review

Motivating Language

Mr. Miller's criteria words for the accounts receivable function are PAID FASTER, REDUCE NON-PAY-MENTS, and SLOW-PAY.

Motivating Direction

He is a mixed pattern, more Away-From than Toward. He spotted two problems—LOSING MONEY and SAVING TIME—and stated them first. But he also sees a goal of growing a business for his kids to benefit from.

Motivating Source

He is an Internal. Although he takes input from other sources, he clearly makes the decision using his own internal criteria.

═══ 5 ═══

Not Being Creative Can Make You Money

Imagine that it's Christmas morning and you have drawn the task of putting together a complicated toy. What do you do once the box is opened and the pieces are out where you can work with them? Do you take a look at the picture on the box and start fitting pieces together, or do you open the instructions and start at Step 1?

Or let's say the toy company gave you the Japanese instructions, or left them out completely, how would you respond? Would you attempt to put the toy together anyway, or would you move on to some other Christmas chore?

The Process Approach

Your reaction to this situation tells a lot about you. It reveals the Process Approach of your HOS program. It describes your operating method: Do you look for procedures to follow or do you seek out new opportunities? We have labeled the patterns elicited by this question as Options and Procedures.

The Options Pattern

A completely Options person wants to expand his possibilities. You may have met people like this: They're the

Category	*Question*
Motivating Language	For you, what is important about *selling*?
Motivating Direction	What do you want *from selling?* What will having *that* really do for you?
Motivating Source	How do you know *that you've done a good job?*
Process Approach	Why did you choose *to be a salesman/woman?*
Decision Strategy	How do you know that *your supplier/accountant/lawyer* is good *at their job?*
Convincer Strategy	How many times do they have to demonstrate this (*that they are good at their job*) before you are convinced?
Process Scope	Tell me about one of your favorite *working experiences.*
Process Relationship	What is the relationship between *what you are doing this year on your job and what you did last year on your job?*

ones who see the opportunity in every situation. They evaluate everything in terms of their criteria (see Chapter 2) and whether it offers them the opportunity to satisfy those criteria. Rules and procedures stymie Options people, although they are quite good at developing those same rules and procedures. The Options person creates a process as a solution, not a rule to live by. He or she abhors routine and often stretches the limits, like getting to work on time. Watch your co-workers; those who consistently come in a few minutes late will almost always turn out to be Options. They are the people who read instructions only as a last resort, and only then because it is just another option for them to try.

The Procedures Pattern

On the other end of the spectrum, a Procedures person feels obliged to follow the rules, to do things in an orderly procedure. He or she feels comfortable as long as there is a system to deal with the situation. This person lives for step-by-step instructions and without them is lost. Procedures people never proceed without reading the instructions. Ironically, as much as they love the step-by-step, they are lousy at making them up. Without a procedure for dealing with things, they become discombobulated and stressed until they get an outlined way of proceeding. Routine is their greatest comfort.

The Question for Process Approach

The following question reveals your Process Approach for the context of being a salesperson. Please answer it for yourself on a sheet of paper or into a tape recorder.

==

WHY DID YOU CHOOSE *to be a sales professional?*

==

How to Interpret What You Hear

Your client's answer to this question will tell you much about them: Do they look for opportunities or do they follow sequences? Do they like routines or abhor them? Will they need the assurance that there is an orderly procedure to your interaction? Through the following sample dialogues you will begin to recognize these two speech patterns and understand just how easy they are to distinguish from each other.

Dialogue A

Alan
(salesman):   I was pleased when we were able to schedule this meeting, Sarah. You may be wondering how our services can do what we say they can. Many of our clients have had similar thoughts before we met. I am curious, Sarah, **WHY DID YOU CHOOSE** *to use an outside vendor for this project?*

Sarah
(client):   Well, Alan, about a year ago the president asked me to head up a project that would deliver a fully integrated information system that could coordinate manufacturing, sales, marketing, and finance into one process. We started with the needs of each department and then examined the correlating aspects of

their needs. After identifying needs and purpose, we identified what talents we had internally. Finally, we determined that to complete a project like this we would either have to hire more talent or go outside on a contract basis. That brings us to this stage of the process.

Dialogue B

Alan: I was pleased when we were able to schedule this meeting, Janet. You may be wondering how our services can do what we say they can. Many of our clients have had similar thoughts before we met. I am curious, Janet, **WHY DID YOU CHOOSE** *to use an outside vendor for this project?*

Janet: Well, Alan, we need a fully integrated information system that will coordinate all our department's activities. We need to cut costs and upgrade our processes to a state-of-the-art system. We don't have the talent internally, so we decided to go outside for help.

What do you notice about these two responses? There are HOS clues everywhere. In Dialogue A, Sarah tells a story; she outlines the procedure her company went through in making their decision. She is focused on methods, steps, and sequence in time: A specific step goes first, then a second one, and so forth. She answers a "why" question with facts: "one year," "president's request," "coordinate manufacturing, sales, marketing, and finance." Then comes the step-by-step breakdown that is so important to the Procedures individual. Actually, Sarah answered the question "How did you choose," not why. When she finishes, you know how she makes decisions, even if you don't know the criteria those decisions are based on. In answering the question "Why did you choose. . . ," a person who describes a process is demonstrating the Procedures pattern. The process is important to them.

Janet, in Dialogue B, doesn't give any facts in her answer. She answers the "why" question with needs and reasons. The response is filled with her criteria for purchase: "fully integrated system," "coordinated departments," "cutting costs and upgrading." You only get a hint of the process they went through in deciding to use an outside vendor. Her answer has no story to it— no people or events or timetables, just criteria that need to be met. Because of that emphasis, her HOS Process Approach is Options.

A few months ago Marvin arranged to meet a potential client at a restaurant. After an initial introduction, Marvin noticed that when asked by the maitre d' whether he had a preference of seating, the client immediately responded, "Well, first I want to make sure that we are away from a high traffic area, and I always sit by a window, and of course, I want to be in a non-smoking area." Marvin closely observed the process with which the man made the decision of where to sit and concluded that he was initially sorting for procedures followed by particular criteria or options backup. To break this down for you, he started with "first I want to make sure that we are away from . . . ," followed by a procedure of how he would choose a seat, and concluded with specific reasons.

Working on the assumption that he had a Procedures pattern, Marvin went on to develop an excellent relationship with this gentleman. He began the conversation by setting up a procedure to follow through lunch and the business discussion. It worked quite well: The man felt comfortable during their conversation and totally aligned with Marvin's presentation. By the end of lunch, he was no longer a potential client; they were doing business together.

Sometimes you do not have to ask the question, all you have to do is observe how an individual responds when interacting with another person. All of us constantly demonstrate the traits cataloged in the Human Operating System program, it is simply a matter of paying attention to the cues. Nonetheless, it is always a good idea to back up your observation by asking the question for that context.

How Process Approach Affects the Sales Cycle

You will use this component of the Human Operating System to impact how you structure your presentation and how you close the sale. With an Options customer, you can bounce around, talking about the many ways your product or service will expand their possibilities. You will certainly stress flexibility and use their criteria words.

If your customer is a Procedures person, your presentation better be well-organized and methodical. It always helps to put forward an outline of the whole presentation beforehand, then be sure to do it in just that order. Remember, step-by-step makes Procedures people feel comfortable. A big advantage of outlining the process is that a Procedures person needs to complete that process. This person won't abandon ship mid-process and go with the next opportunity presented.

Procedures people tend to distrust Options people, something you need to be aware of if you're an Options person selling to a Procedures customer. On the other hand, Options think of Procedures as dull and inflexible. If you're having that feeling about your client, modify your approach by breaking your presentation into steps.

Pre-Closing Sarah, The Procedures Buyer

Remember, Procedures people distrust those who bring them unstructured presentations or materials. For them, interactions must have a beginning, middle, and end. With a client like Sarah, you must either fit into her sequence or create one for her to follow. For Procedures customers, the primary considerations are identifying the process and completing it. If they seem to waver, respond by breaking things down into steps: You might explain the process of getting it from the plant to their door, for instance. Whatever you do, don't give them new options, such as more benefits, further comparisons, expansive possibilities. That may excite you, but Procedures people operate most effectively within known options. They become lost without a planned course of action. As we said, they follow the rules and instinctively distrust anyone who does not.

Here's how Alan responded to Sarah's description of their vendor selection process:

> *Alan:*   That sounds like a very logical way to make a decision. Before I get started with my presentation, I want to outline what I'm going to do. **First**, I will go over your specific needs. **Second**, I will explain how our services work and the types of projects we have completed. **The third step** will be the integration of how we would handle your project and the additional value-added benefits you will receive. **Fourth**, all your questions will be addressed and any additional information you need will be provided. And **finally**, our fees will be agreed on according to your budget requirements

so that an agreement can be authorized. Oh, I almost forgot, it is my **procedure** to take you to lunch a few days before we begin in order to celebrate our agreement and to insure that we are on track. By the way, what kind of food do you like to eat?

Sarah: I like to eat healthy, so something light would be my preference.

Alan: Great, I know an excellent place. Well, Sarah, let's get started.

We have highlighted the steps so you can see how easy it is to "procedure-ize" things. You don't need to emphasize the steps with your voice: The customer's response to them is unconscious.

Pre-Selling Janet, The Options Buyer

Listen closely to the words and phrases the Options person uses: In answering your why question, she is telling you her criteria words. They may even be the same words used to answer the Motivating Language question in Chapter 2. Those words represent her values, what she is looking for, and you must match them if you want to make the sale. Whatever else you do, remember those words.

An Options person will explain her choices in terms of opportunities—to learn, to make money, to improve, to get a free meal, to meet someone new, or to upgrade the system. Options people are motivated to expand their horizons, so they respond when benefits are couched as possibilities. Given a choice between following procedures and exploring new territory, they will always choose to explore.

You should talk to them about "why" your product is better. Use their criteria words often. Never discuss "how" with them. Procedures limit them, and they do not respond to limitations. For example, the instant you start to talk about the process of filling the order—the contracts, the shippers, the bills of lading, the nuts and bolts of making it work—they lose interest and you lose the deal.

Here's Alan's response to Janet's list of criteria words:

> **Alan:** Good, it sounds as if you have a number of activities to satisfy. It is our practice to provide enough options for our clients so they can go in a NUMBER OF DIRECTIONS to meet their goals. The results of our services can provide you with a track to follow that includes many feeder lines, so to speak. You're going to have CHOICES so the real challenges of this project aren't missed.

As with any continuum of behavior, few people are going to be wholly Options or Procedures, but for the most part, one or the other pattern will predominate. Your clients will continually demonstrate their preferred patterns through speech cues that will become as obvious to you as the noses on their faces once you are used to listening for them. When you have delineated their patterns, adjust your presentation accordingly.

HINT

An easy way to remember the distinction between Options and Procedures is to think of instructions:

When putting something together, an Options person dives in and only reads the instructions once he or she has failed at least once to put it together.

A Procedures person will not begin the project without reading the instructions. If no instructions are available, they will not attempt to put it together.

Spend a few days asking only this question from the HOS Profile. This is the best way to learn to evaluate the responses. It won't take many examples of each pattern before you can quickly distinguish between them.

What Is Your Process Approach?

Where do you fall on the spectrum between Options and Procedures? Did you answer a "how" question or "why"? Did you outline a scenario with facts ("I answered an ad, interviewed, trained, and got the job")? Or did you describe the opportunities your current job offers ("It was a golden opportunity to increase my income, to work with people I liked")? Did you step through a procedure? Or did you reel off criteria?

Go to pages 163–164 and mark the appropriate box on the Process Approach line of the HOS Profile Chart.

Practice Makes Perfect

The patterns for Process Approach are simple to decipher: Does the person answer with criteria or facts? Do they answer a "how" question or a "why"? Pick out the patterns in these examples. Answers appear on pages 67–69.

Bill: Alice, you really like the car you bought last year. I'm wondering, why did you choose that particular model?

Alice: It really looked great and the price was right.

Example 2

Bill: Jim, I can tell you really like your new car. I was wondering, why did you choose that particular model?

Jim: Last year when I was looking for a car, I must have visited ten different dealerships. I collected lots of information, but it came down to two sporty models at two different dealers. The clincher came when the sales manager showed me his numbers compared to the other dealer. When that happened, it seemed right to make a decision.

Example 3

Karla: Buying a home is a decision that will have lasting effects. We talked about the last home you purchased, and I'm curious about why you chose to buy that one?

Michelle: As I told you earlier, the reason was that it fit our pocketbook, and it was in a location that had good schools for the kids. It was also important that the commute to work was convenient for both my husband and me.

Example 4

> *Karla:*   Buying a home is a decision that will have lasting effects. We talked about the last home you purchased, and I'm curious about why you chose to buy that one?

> *Tom:*   It's really a long story. It started about eight months before. My wife and I saw the house being built. We lived on the other side of town and wanted to move to that area. We stopped to talk with the builder, and he kept our name. About six months later, the builder called and told us that the people he'd been building it for couldn't close. We put a contract on it immediately.

Reviewing further is essential in learning how to distinguish the patterns in Process Approach. We suggest that you ask this question, in a variety of contexts, of people who will let you record their answers on tape. At home, play their answers until you are sure whether they give you criteria or tell you the procedure they went through to arrive at their decision.

Answers to the Review

Example 1

> *Alice:*   It really LOOKED GREAT and THE PRICE WAS RIGHT.

Alice is Options; she answers with her criteria for purchase.

Example 2

> *Jim:*   Last year when I was looking for a car, I must have visited ten different dealerships. I collected lots of information, but it came down to two sporty models at two different dealers. The clincher came when the sales manager showed me his numbers compared to the other dealer. When that happened, it seemed right to make a decision.

Jim is Procedures because he answers with a story that tells *how* he made his decision.

Example 3

> *Michelle:*   As I told you earlier, the reason was that it FIT OUR POCKETBOOK, and it was in a LOCATION THAT HAD GOOD SCHOOLS for the kids. It was also important that the COMMUTE TO WORK WAS CONVENIENT for both my husband and me.

Michelle is Options because she tells us what's important to her about the house she bought.

Example 4

> *Tom:*   It's really a long story. It started about eight months before. My wife and I saw the house being built. We lived on the other side of town and wanted to move to that area. We stopped to talk with the builder, and he kept our name. About six

months later, he called and told us that the people he'd been building it for couldn't close. We put a contract on it immediately.

Tom is Procedures because he tells a story that begins at the beginning and then moves sequentially through time to a conclusion. He does throw in one phrase of criteria, and that is that he and his wife wanted to move to that area.

6

TALKING YOUR WAY OUT OF SALES

A friend who owns a printing company related this story:

He was awaiting a government contract for $3-$4 million in business. In order to obtain this contract, a government inspector had to come by his plant to review a production sample. The inspector arrived about mid-day, and they decided to have lunch before looking at the samples. Right after lunch the printing company owner and the inspector went into a gift shop near where they had eaten in Fort Worth, Texas, which is known in the Lone Star State as Cow Town. The inspector wanted to buy his son a cowboy belt to take back to Washington, D.C. While in the gift shop, our friend was able to observe the inspector's Decision Strategy.

The man went to a belt rack and removed a belt; he looked at it on the inside and on the outside, put it back and pulled a second belt. He scrutinized that belt intently, examining all of the seam work, put it back and pulled a third belt from the rack. He looked closely at the stitching and the craftsmanship, and then went to the counter and purchased that belt. By observing that behavior, my printer friend determined that the inspector from Washington, D.C. made decisions visually.

When they returned to his plant for the inspection, the owner took great pains to show the inspector all the detail of the printing process. He pointed out the craftsmanship

Category	*Question*
Motivating Language	For you, what is important about *selling?*
Motivating Direction	What do you want *from selling?* What will having *that* really do for you?
Motivating Source	How do you know *that you've done a good job?*
Process Approach	Why did you choose *to be a salesman/woman?*
Decision Strategy	How do you know that *your supplier/accountant/lawyer* is good *at their job?*
Convincer Strategy	How many times do they have to demonstrate this (*that they are good at their job*) before you are convinced?
Process Scope	Tell me about one of your favorite *working experiences.*
Process Relationship	What is the relationship between *what you are doing this year on your job* and *what you did last year on your job?*

in the color mixing in the pictures and presented his product in a very visual manner. I will finish this story in the next chapter on Convincer Strategy, but I wanted to use it here to illustrate it is important to notice how people make decisions. By the way, they did sign a contract that day for the printing project.

Decision Strategy

Just as a DOS program orients the computer to accept data through the keyboard, an optical scanner, or a floppy disk, so your individual HOS program orients your brain to take in data through your eyes, ears, or feelings. (From the standpoint of pure utility in the modern world, at least, smell and taste are essentially peripheral senses.) Every person has a Decision Strategy, favoring one sensory channel over the other two. We call this Decision Strategy because it is crucial to how we decide everything. Yet, basic as this is to the way we act, react, and interact, few people know how to decipher it consistently.

Knowing a person's Decision Strategy is a potent piece of data in creating relationships. It allows us to give others information in the way they are predisposed to receiving it. The possible patterns are Visual, Auditory, and Feelings (some people prefer to call Feelings "*Kinesthetic*").

Visual

As you would expect, Visual people primarily learn and are convinced by seeing things done. They prefer to take in information by observing; they are most at home with pictures, graphs, and other forms of visual data. They tend to ignore or delete much of the information presented in other ways. Hand them a brochure while you're speaking and their attention will go immediately to the paper, and you will have lost them to what you are saying. People with the visual pattern may like to read information as well as see images. The desire to read demonstrates a visual preference. Many people you meet (about 70 percent) will be visually oriented, just because visual stimulation begins at such an early age. The television has influenced many Decision Strategy patterns.

Auditory

Auditory people listen and tend to ignore or delete information that is not spoken. Hand an auditory a sheet of paper while you're talking, and he won't even glance at it. This Decision Strategy is found in approximately twenty-five percent of the population.

Feelings

Feelings people are hands-on and must do a task to learn it. They value the experience of doing it over seeing it done or hearing about it. In fact, they often disregard information presented in those ways. Feelings people comprise the remaining five percent of the population.

In addition to these three categories, there is some mixing. There are people who are both Visual and Auditory, others who are Auditory and Feelings, others Feelings and Visual. Even in cases of combined preferences, however, one sensory system is typically preferred over the other.

We want to make it clear that it is not that a Visual person cannot hear, rather they are "over-sighted": They simply depend more on visual cues and stimulation than other forms of communication. The same is true for Auditory and Feelings people. Think about how people learn in a school context: Some are perfectly happy with a pure lecture format (Auditory); others really need to have slides or a video presentation in order to understand (Visual); and still others learn best when they can actually do something, like attend a lab. Each of us concentrates most easily and is most attentive when using our preferred sensory channel. No one consciously decides his Decision Strategy: Our preferences are established very early in life, most likely within the first six months.

The Question for Decision Strategy

The following question reveals your Decision Strategy. Please answer it for yourself on a sheet of paper or into a tape recorder.

HOW DO YOU KNOW THAT *your supplier/accountant/ lawyer/a co-worker* **IS GOOD** *at their job?*

How to Interpret What You Hear

Our language is full of cues to our Decision Strategy, but you will hear it most clearly in the verbs people select when answering this question.

Visual

A Visual person will answer the Decision Strategy question like this: "I see them do their work." "Through observation." "I watch what they do and look at the results." "They have to show me they know what they're doing."

Visual people talk about the world and their experience in visual words and phrases. They focus and view and observe. Asked to recall a mountain scene, they will describe the deep green forest dappled in light, the crystal clear water reflecting a cloudless blue sky. They live in a world of sight relationships. They look for information.

Auditory

Auditory people answer the question with sound verbs: "I ask questions, and they tell me what they know." "We talk." "I hear how they're doing from the people they work with." "I know he's good at his job because he puts it in layman's terms when he explains it to you."

An Auditory person listens and keeps his or her ears open and asks questions that others respond to verbally. From the mountain scene, they will remark on the sound of the water, the bird songs, and the wind in the trees. When they talk about their experience, which Auditory people will do quite readily, they will use verbs like those. They live in a world of sound relationships. They listen for information.

Feelings

Feelings people answer the co-worker question like this: "I have to work with them." "We must develop it together." "I know he's good at his job because he does it the way I do it."

The language of a Feelings person is full of references to doing things. They work with and follow and do. They will recall the temperature of the day and the water at the mountain stream, how heavy the rocks were, and whether they were slippery. They live in a world of spatial and tactile relationships.

How Decision Strategy Affects the Sales Cycle

Many communications problems arise because of mismatched Decision Strategies. For example, when an Auditory salesperson "tells" a Visual prospect the benefits of the product, or tries to close that person over the phone, he or she creates a barrier instead of a bridge. Because the salesperson is convinced by hearing things, he or she unconsciously assumes that everyone is convinced the same way. When a customer's attention starts to wane, this person typically responds by increasing the word-count or volume or both. Of course, that causes the visual prospect to glaze over even more. What is needed in that situation is less tell and more show—visual aids, photographs, brochures, charts, or pretty pictures and minimal phone contact.

A friend recently told us how she observed Decision Strategies working out in her office.

Her boss, Bill, bought a new computer program for the telemarketing division. The salesperson showed him all sorts of information, including an impressively illustrated operating manual. A classic Visual, Bill bought the package, but not the optional classroom training: He felt confident his team could learn the program from the book. It looked straightforward, and there were lots of pictures.

Unfortunately, his staff was primarily Auditory (as telemarketers naturally tend to be) and had difficulty learning from books. They needed to hear how the program worked. They needed to ask questions and listen to instructions put in a variety of terms. They needed things "worded" and re-worded. From their standpoint, the best the book could do was supplement verbal training. After a week of struggling with the "incredibly clear and simple" (Bill's words) instruction manual, the telemarketing division was essentially at a standstill. Desperate and mystified, Visual Bill agreed to purchase the optional training. Within half a day, everyone in the office was fluent in the program.

As a salesperson, your job is to convince people that your product or service is the best one available. Matching their Decision Strategy is the first step in that process. When you can deliver your information to your customers on their most active sensory channel, you will begin to sell the way they buy. Delivering your message through unused channels results in frustration and failure.

Using Decision Strategies to Pre-Sell Your Client

Now that you know the distinctions among the three Decision Strategies, you will easily spot them in conversation. Your evaluation of your client's sensory preference should color your whole presentation. Do not make the common mistake of giving information the way you like to receive it. Adapt your language and your presentation to your audience, and fatter commission checks will be your reward.

Pre-Selling the Visual Customer

Part of gaining rapport with a Visual person involves using visual language. Don't say, "I understand what you're saying"; instead agree by saying "I see what you mean." On the phone, make word pictures. When you visit them, take plenty of visual props and show them liberally: These customers will absorb that visual information more effectively than any words you speak.

Don't be offended if they pay more attention to your props than to you. As you talk to them, invite them to "look things over" and "see" for themselves. If you are Visual, you will naturally use these phrases, but if you are not, you will increase your ability to communicate with Visual people by getting familiar with the list of visual verbs at the end of this chapter.

Pre-Selling the Auditory Customer

Gaining rapport with Auditory people begins by using their sensory verbs. Say things like "I hear what you're saying" instead of "I see what you mean." Rather than "Let's get together," "Let's talk Friday." "Let me tell you about . . . ," not "Let me show you our newest. . . ."

When making a sales call to an Auditory, it isn't necessary to bring along your visual aids: For the most part, they won't look at them unless you explain them. Even then they are unlikely to recall them or give them much weight in their final decision. At most times, they are comfortable with phone contact, and they often like to talk. If you are Visual, you will want to familiarize yourself with the Auditory verbs at the end of this chapter.

Pre-Selling the Feelings Customer

Calling on a Feelings client requires you to match their hands-on style of learning. This can often be challenging to Visual and Auditory people. Be sure to have props that they can touch and hold, even if it's nothing more than a give-away pen. Fiddling with things helps them take in and sort information. They won't necessarily watch you nor seem to be listening at times, but they will be taking it in.

When talking to a Feelings prospect, focus on action verbs and the activities involved in what your company does or makes. They are very spatially aware, so be liberal with dimensions and locations: "Our offices are at the corner of Ledbetter and Hawthorne. Come and visit us. Once we've walked through the plant together, you'll know how we do things." Emphasize how much you want "to work with them," "to track down the problems and develop solutions," and "do it just the way you would do it."

It probably seems like we're overemphasizing something as seemingly trivial as the verbs you use in a sentence, but we're not. Rapport is a very subtle and unconscious experience. The accumulation of these "trivial" events is what creates affinity between people. If you look at things the way I look at things, or hear them the way I hear them, or do them the way I do them—I can trust you more than those who see or hear or do those same things differently. When you match a person's sensory preference, they intuit your alignment with their perception of the world, just as when you match their criteria words, they instinctively believe you understand what they want. The more conscious you can become of the unconscious components that make up rapport, the more likely you will create it consciously in your relationships.

To convince yourself how easy and accurate this is, we suggest that you spend several days just asking this one question—"How do you know that someone (a specific person) is good at their job?"—of as many people as you can. At first, it may appear impossible to isolate a few phrases from what will likely seem a torrent of words, but it's easy. You will quickly develop the ability to hear and evaluate the clues to Decision Strategy. Once you know a person's style, use the appropriate language in your conversation. Then, intentionally mismatch them and observe, listen, or feel any changes in the quality of the interaction. Within a very short time, you will be able to discern Decision Strategy in normal speech and will no longer need to ask the question.

Alternative Questions

You may not always be able to ask the question exactly as posed at the beginning of this chapter. You can ask the question in several ways, but the object of the question must always be another person, never the prospect. If you ask the customer how he knows he's good at his own job, you'll learn his Motivating Source, not his Decision Strategy. Also, you must word the question in such a way that they have to tell you about a specific person and not refer to abstract qualities. Following are examples that may fit more easily into the selling environment. The **boldfaced** words are the significant ones; you may fill in the *italicized* words with the context that interests you, i.e., vendor, product, boss, relationships, etc.

HOW DID YOU KNOW *your last supplier*
DID A GOOD JOB?

The last person that sold you a product,
HOW DID YOU KNOW THEY DID A GOOD JOB?
HOW DO YOU KNOW *that your employees are doing*
A GOOD JOB?

What Is Your Decision Strategy?

How did you answer the question "How do you know that your supplier/accountant/lawyer/co-worker is good at their job?" Are you Visual, Auditory, or Feelings? The odds are that you are Visual, but there are millions of people in the other two categories, and many more who combine two. Record your Decision Strategy on pages 163–164 by marking the appropriate box in the HOS Profile Chart.

LISTS OF VERBS

VISUAL	AUDITORY	FEELINGS
SEE	HEAR	TOUCH
LOOK	LISTEN	HANDLE
FOCUS	TELL	GRASP
SHOW	DOUBLE TALK	ROUGH
GLANCE	TALK	SMOOTH
STARE	SPEAK	EXCITED
PREVIEW	GRUMBLE	IMPACT
SHORT-SIGHTED	RINGS TRUE	HIT ON
CLARIFY	SOUNDS GOOD TO ME	TENDER
GRAPHIC	SOUNDS LIKE	GRAB
COLOR	WHAT I HEAR	STROKE
FRAME	TUNE IN	GET THE POINT
VISUALIZE	HARMONY	CUT UP
DRESS UP	GIVE AN EAR	SCARED
FORESEE	GIVE A LISTEN	ANGRY
KEEN	UNHEARD OF	HOT
CLOUD	EARFUL	TOUGH
DARK	VOLUME	SOLID
FANTASIZE	ALL EARS	BOUNCE
HORIZON	SAY ANYTHING	IRRITATE
OVERVIEW	WORD OF MOUTH	LUKEWARM

Practice Makes Perfect

The patterns for Decision Strategy quickly become clear as you tune your own perception to hearing them in other people's speech: What verbs and figures of speech do they put into their conversation? Do they see, hear, or feel? Answers appear on pages 84–85.

Example 1

Paul: Anne, you've worked with a consultant before in your company. I was wondering how you knew that they were doing a good job.

Anne: That was easy. All I had to do was listen to the feedback from the production department.

Example 2

Bruce: Earlier you mentioned that you had worked with a consultant before and had been satisfied with their work. I was wondering how you knew that they had done a good job?

Paula: They were always here on time and when I talked to them, they could explain to me in detail what they were doing. I just got the feeling that they knew their stuff.

Example 3

Carol: Based on your present relationship, Bret, how did you know that Sue was really intent on making it work?

Bret: When we get together, we just seem to blend into each other's thoughts.

Example 4

Linda: How do you know that you've got a good relationship?

Janice: I really notice how he talks to me and the things he does for me. I get lots of cards, for no special reason. And I can read the depth of his feelings in the messages. This boy is for real.

Reviewing further is essential to learning how to distinguish the patterns in Decision Strategy. We suggest you ask this question, in a variety of contexts, of anyone who will let you record their answer on tape. At home, play their answers until you are sure whether they are Visual, Auditory, or Feelings.

Answers to the Review

Example 1

Anne: That was easy. All I had to do was LISTEN TO THE FEEDBACK from the production department.

Anne is Auditory.

Example 2

Paula: They were always HERE ON TIME and when I TALKED TO THEM, they could EXPLAIN to me in detail what they were doing. I just GOT THE FEELING that they knew their stuff.

Paula has a mixed preference, both Auditory and Feelings. "Here on time" demonstrates that she prefers to do things with people and is a Feelings cue, as is "got the feeling."

Example 3

> *Bret:* When we GET TOGETHER, we just seem to BLEND INTO each other's thoughts.

Bret is Feelings.

Example 4

> *Janice:* I really NOTICE the things he does for me and how he TALKS to me. I get lots of cards, for no special reason. And I can READ the depth of his feelings in the messages. This boy is for real.

Janice is another mixed preference, Visual and Auditory.

IS IT *REALLY* WHAT YOU SAY THAT CONVINCES YOUR CUSTOMER?

You know that making a sale is nothing more than convincing your customer that you have what they need. What complicates this simple truth is this reality: Every person becomes convinced in a different way. Each of us has a strategy by which we make decisions within a given context, whether it's choosing a car or choosing a stall in a public restroom. The Convincer Strategy is the means by which we decide, because it lets us know whether or not our criteria are met. When you move a customer to decision, you have met the requirements of his or her Convincer Strategy.

We each have our own method, and though it is unconscious, we know exactly what it is and whether or not it has been met. Knowing how your prospects are convinced will save you untold anxiety. This knowledge will keep you from bothering them for an answer because you will know when they are ready to decide.

Convincer Strategies

This part of the Human Operating System comprises four patterns: Automatic, Consistent, Number of Examples, and Time Period. These four patterns are simple to

Category	*Question*
Motivating Language	For you, what is important about *selling*?
Motivating Direction	What do you want *from selling?* What will having *that* really do for you?
Motivating Source	How do you know *that you've done a good job*?
Process Approach	Why did you choose *to be a salesman/woman*?
Decision Strategy	How do you know that *your supplier/accountant/lawyer* is good *at their job*?
Convincer Strategy	How many times do they have to demonstrate this (*that they are good at their job*) before you are convinced?
Process Scope	Tell me about one of your favorite *working experiences*.
Process Relationship	What is the relationship between *what you are doing this year on your job and what you did last year on your job*?

distinguish from one another and easy to recognize, as you will discover.

Automatic

Most people would characterize an Automatic as someone "who jumps right in." This person doesn't need to have seen, heard, or done a thing to believe that he or she can do it. This person has a high trust level. As an example, an Automatic shopper never compares prices or checks out other brands. If he or she wants a radio, for instance, the first radio seen will suit just fine. Essentially, Automatics need no proof because they are automatically convinced.

Consistent

The Consistent pattern is exactly opposite the Automatic. This person has a low level of trust. A Consistent evaluates constantly: Just because Cafe Noir was good last week doesn't mean it will be good tonight. This person is, essentially, never convinced. Every day is a new day. Consistents typically hold no preconceived notions and require regular reconvincing. As clients, they can be frustrating because they won't cut you much slack or let you rest on your laurels. In the shopping example, a Consistent would need to check out several sources before buying a radio and even then may not be convinced until he or she uses the product for some time.

Number of Examples

A Number of Examples person needs to see, hear, or do something a certain number of times to be convinced. The number varies from person to person, of course, but an Examples person will always answer the question with a specific number. It may be one, it may be two, it may be twenty, but it is the magic number. Attempting to make them decide before they have had the requisite number of examples will only irritate them and frustrate you. A 3-Example person buying cat food needs to evaluate three different samples—either brands, sizes, or flavors—before deciding.

Time Period

People with the Time Period pattern require a time interval before they decide. They are specific about that interval: It may be two hours, two days, two weeks, or longer. No matter how short or long the interval, Time Period people must have that amount of time or they will not be convinced.

The Question for Convincer Strategy

The question for Convincer Strategy relates to the previous one, "How do you know that someone is good at their job?" Please answer it on a sheet of paper or into a tape recorder.

HOW MANY TIMES DO THEY HAVE TO DEMONSTRATE THIS

(that they are good at their job) **BEFORE YOU ARE CONVINCED?**

How to Interpret What You Hear

This is among the easiest patterns to distinguish in response to the question. Even though their Convincer

Strategy is in the deep background of the Human Operating System, people's answers slide off their tongues as if they'd been waiting for this one question all their lives.

An Automatic will respond with answers like these: "I give people the benefit of the doubt." "I assume they're good at their job or they wouldn't be in it." "I just have to see them do it and I know whether they can." "I just trust that people can do the job."

Consistent individuals respond in this way: "I never believe someone's good at their job, they have to show me every day." "Just because they can do it today doesn't mean they can do it tomorrow." "Things change." "You can't count on people to be consistent."

Examples people always answer with a number: "I have to see him to do it four times, then I know." "If you hear from five different people that they know what they're doing, you can be pretty sure they do." "After I've done it with them twice, I can tell."

Even though the question is worded for a Number-of-Examples answer, Time Period people respond as if the question were "how long do they have to demonstrate?" They respond like this: "It takes me a couple of days of working with them to know for sure." "If I can watch them for two hours, I'll always know." "If I don't hear any complaints for a week, they know what they're doing."

How Convincer Strategy Affects the Sales Cycle

Convincer Strategies are crucial to decision-making. Decision Strategy and Convincer Strategy together give you vital input about how a person takes in information and how he or she processes it to decide. Knowing this gives you a big advantage because it allows you to give your customer information in a way and in proportions that remove obstacles to making decisions. Let's take as an illustration a person who is Visual/5-Examples.

It is not necessary to make five separate sales calls to persuade the client to buy from you. After your initial call, you can send four different mailings relating to your product. Or you may break one sales call into five examples by taking along visual props that you can bring out one at a time. That can add up to the magic five-count.

As another example, let's take a prospect who is Auditory/Time-2 Weeks. Once you have made the initial call, you can wait patiently, or you can make a couple of courtesy calls in the interim to ensure that you stay on the list. Whatever you do, don't contact this person with the expectation of an order then. Just be patient for two weeks and you'll do your case a lot more good.

If you are the impatient type, however, you can speed up the process.

Marvin once had to sell to a man whose Convincer Strategy was six months. You can be sure many salesmen gave up in frustration long before they got an answer. Marvin didn't want to wait that long, however, so he arranged for his HOS program to think that amount of time passed. During the sales call, he asked him to recall what he was doing six months before: The man named off several things. At that point, Marvin made the sales presentation again. The client laughed, saying he had already seen it. Marvin put the presentation away and started bringing him forward in time by talking about things that had happened in the interim until they were once again in the present. Then he showed the presentation again, saying, "I showed you this presentation six months ago, what do you think about it?" He laughed because they both knew it was a game, but his HOS program didn't. It associated the presentation with six months previous, and he bought the program that day.

In the case of a Consistent client, being forewarned is being forearmed. Be prepared to prove yourself and your wares every time you go in. Be consistent in everything you do with them: Be on time, follow through on what you say you will do when you say you'll do it, and don't substitute things you've promised. In other words, be ready to be put through your paces. They are unlikely ever to cut you any slack. One boo-boo and you can be history. For a Consistent, inconsistency is practically intolerable.

One chink in this armor is that a Consistent has never bought anything he or she was completely convinced was perfect. You can play to that by recalling some earlier buying experience—"Remember when you bought your color television set?"—and then say something like "This is just like that. You won't be convinced until you buy it and try it out."

The key to selling to Automatics is creating rapport and building trust. A crucial step in that process is matching their Decision Strategy in your language. Use the other means of creating rapport that we have outlined and an Automatic will trust you. If you match all their HOS components, and they need your product, they will buy from you.

One problem does occur occasionally in selling to Automatics: If you or your product in any way resembles or reminds them of someone or something that they don't trust, they will automatically associate you with that person or product.

After you've practiced identifying Decision Strategies, add the Convincer Strategy question to get the full range of information about how a person learns, is convinced, and decides. Once you have them pegged, think of creative ways to match their Convincer Strategy and move them to a decision. Practice on everyone. Attempt to convince them to go to your favorite restaurant or to a particular movie. Challenge yourself to give them what they need in order to make the decision you want them to make.

Alternative Question

HOW MANY TIMES DO OTHERS *have to be successful*
BEFORE YOU ARE CONVINCED *they know what they're doing?*

What Is Your Convincer Strategy?

How did you answer the question? Are you Automatic, Consistent, Examples, or Time Period? Record the Convincer Strategy of your HOS Profile Chart on pages 163–164 by marking the appropriate box. Understand your HOS Profile so you can prevent yourself from assuming that everyone thinks alike. Knowing your own HOS Profile gives you the freedom to match the person you are addressing.

At this point, we would like to complete the story from the previous chapter regarding the printing company owner and the inspector from Washington, D.C. You may recall that while the inspector was purchasing the belt for his son he looked at three belts, indicating to the printer, who was a keen observer of HOS cues, that the inspector was Visual/3-Examples. When they returned to the plant, the owner showed the inspector the printing results three separate times while pointing out how the quality matched the specific criteria within their request for proposal. The sale was completed before the inspector left town and the contract was initiated.

People know what convinces them, and they remain unconvinced until that criterion is met. Knowing a person's Convincer Strategy will save you untold aggravation in giving your clients information in exactly the manner that convinces them.

Practice Makes Perfect

The patterns for Convincer Strategy are simple to decipher: Does the person answer with a number or a time period? Do they trust easily or do they withhold trust in lieu of a consistent performance? Answers appear on pages 97–98.

Example 1

Madison: Working with a lawyer on critical cases, you have to have a trusting relationship. How many times did he have to do a good job before you were convinced that he was a good attorney?

Roger: You're right. When you're in court, your future depends on that person and whether he can support you professionally. How long? Let me see, probably the third time he presented a case I could tell. After that I knew he could do a good job for us.

Example 2

Lynn: I have had such a hard time finding a doctor, and you seem so pleased with yours. How many times did she have to demonstrate that she was a good doctor before you were convinced?

Shirley: My doctor? She has to prove it every time. Things change too fast in that profession, and so do I. My condition is different every day. She just doesn't get to rest on her laurels. I just can't treat my health like that.

Example 3

Marc: You have worked with brokers before and had some good relationships. How often would he have to do a good job for you before you really trusted him?

Judy: I've worked with three brokers over the last five years, and I knew they were good when I gave them my money to invest. I wouldn't have worked with them if I hadn't thought they knew their business.

Example 4

Leroy: I've got a pile of dirty shirts up to my knees because I just can't find a cleaner that I can trust. I'm beginning to think that I'm unreasonable. Tell me, Tara, how many times do you think somebody has to do a good job before you're convinced?

Tara: It just takes time, Leroy. I figure about four months, and if they haven't done anything wrong, then they probably know what they're doing, and you don't have to worry anymore.

Reviewing further is essential in learning how to distinguish the Convincer Strategy patterns. We suggest you ask this question, in a variety of contexts, of anyone who will let you record their answer on tape. At home, play their answers until you are sure whether they are giving you a time frame, a number of examples, are automatically convinced, or are never convinced.

Answers to the Review

Example 1

Roger: You're right. When you're in court, your future depends on that person and whether he can support you professionally. How long? Let me see, probably the THIRD TIME he presented a case I could tell. After that I knew he could do a good job for us.

Roger is 3-Examples.

Example 2

Shirley: My doctor? She has to PROVE IT EVERY TIME. Things change too fast in that profession, and so do I. MY CONDITION IS DIFFERENT EVERY DAY. She just DOESN'T GET TO REST ON HER LAURELS. I just can't treat my health like that.

Shirley is Consistent.

Example 3

> *Judy:*   I've worked with three brokers over the last five years, and I KNEW THEY WERE GOOD WHEN I GAVE THEM MY MONEY TO INVEST. I WOULDN'T HAVE WORKED WITH THEM IF I HADN'T THOUGHT THEY KNEW THEIR BUSINESS.

Judy is Automatic; she knows going in and doesn't need to be convinced.

Example 4

> *Tara:*   It just TAKES TIME, Leroy. I figure ABOUT FOUR MONTHS, and if they haven't done anything wrong, then they probably know what they're doing, and you don't have to worry anymore.

Tara is Time-4 Months.

Review of Chapters 5, 6, & 7

Huggins, the consultant, calls Miller, his potential customer. Can you decipher his HOS Profile for Process Approach, Decision Strategy, and Convincer Strategy?

Huggins: Good afternoon, Mr. Miller. I am calling you as you requested to confirm a time to meet with your accounts receivable manager. Is he okay for the middle of the week?

Miller: Yes, Thursday morning will be fine for him, and I will be available on and off during the day to meet with you.

Huggins: By the way, Mr. Miller, I forgot to ask you a question while I was there. I am curious why you chose the consultants you used last time.

Miller: Well, Mr. Huggins, I think I mentioned that before, that they were good at what they did and they answered all my questions satisfactorily. They also had great references.

Huggins: Great, that answers my question. Shall I ask for you when I arrive on Thursday morning?

Miller: Yes, can you be here at 7:30 A.M. so we can talk a little more before I set you up with the manager?

Huggins: Sure, I'll be there at 7:30 A.M. Do you want me to bring some donuts?

Miller: I'll tell you what, mix and match some pastries, and I'll supply the coffee.

Huggins: Sounds great, I'll make sure we have plenty of choices. I'll be there Thursday.

Thursday morning arrives.

Huggins: Good morning, Mr. Miller. I was tempted to eat these pastries, but I thought I had better give you first choice.

Miller: I appreciate that. Let's have coffee in my office. There are a few things I want you to know before you meet the manager.

Huggins: Mr. Miller, when you used the other consulting firm, how did you know they were doing a good job when they were in your operation?

Miller: That was pretty easy to tell. The meetings we had after each day told me that they understood my business and could get to the heart of the problems. Also, the employees gave me good feedback. The end result, of course, was a system that works. I didn't hear one complaint about the new process after they left.

Huggins: Great. Well, what do you want to tell me before we meet the manager?

Miller: This is strictly confidential. I would like you to evaluate whether you think the manager is capable of handling accounts receivable at the level it is growing. Can you give me some feedback on that before you leave today?

Huggins: I will be glad to tell you what I think.

Miller: Thanks. By the way, why didn't you get some pastries with apple filling? Those are my favorite.

Huggins: I'll remember that the next time we meet. I want to compliment you on your assistant. She is really professional and knows her business well.

Miller: She has worked for me about two years and probably could handle my job.

Huggins: I hired a research person about a month ago, and finding people you can depend on these days is getting to be a big challenge. I'm wondering, how often do you think a person has to do a good job before you are convinced they are capable?

Miller:	You may find this hard to believe, Mr. Huggins, but I can tell almost immediately. I knew my assistant would be good when I finished interviewing her.
Huggins:	I guess I felt that way, too, but you know, there are times when I question myself. I guess that keeps us on our toes.
Miller:	You're right about that. Now let's go meet the manager and put you to work.

Answers to the Review

Process Approach

Mr. Miller is Options. He answered completely with criteria words and no procedure. He answered a why question.

Decision Strategy

He is Auditory. He knows because he hears it said.

Convincer Strategy

He is Automatic. He knows immediately.

====== 8 ======

When to Talk *Too* Much

Have you ever noticed how differently people eat? Some people cut their food into small pieces, while others hardly use a knife at all and gulp huge mouthfuls.

Process Scope

We are like that about how we take in information. Some people like it in small, bite-sized pieces, while others prefer big chunks. When you know your client's "Process Scope," it's easy to give your sales presentation in just the chunk size the client likes.

Process Scope consists of a continuum between two patterns: General and Specific.

General

The General person concentrates on the big picture and works best when he or she can delegate the details. This person tends to look at the world through a wide-angle lens. These individuals are most comfortable at the concept level and struggle to follow the step-by-step procedures required to bring a project to completion. To them, the parts of a system are unrelated, a random set. Details are easily overlooked when giving directions and easily forgotten when receiving them.

Category	Question
Motivating Language	For you, what is important about *selling*?
Motivating Direction	What do you want *from selling*? What will having *that* really do for you?
Motivating Source	How do you know *that you've done a good job*?
Process Approach	Why did you choose *to be a salesman/woman*?
Decision Strategy	How do you know that *your supplier/accountant/lawyer* is good *at their job*?
Convincer Strategy	How many times do they have to demonstrate this (*that they are good at their job*) before you are convinced?
Process Scope	Tell me about one of your favorite *working experiences*.
Process Relationship	What is the relationship between *what you are doing this year on your job and what you did last year on your job*?

Specific

If the General uses a wide-angle lens, the Specific uses a microscopic one. He or she will only see the whole picture when it is loaded with details. Often, this person is so focused on the immediate task that he or she does not conceive of how it relates to a larger goal. This person defines tasks in terms of sequences, not purposes: "I do this, then this, then that," not "I do this because it's required for my taxes." If this person doesn't develop a detailed plan for a task, or doesn't get one from someone else, he or she will be lost and won't begin to work. To a person who is fully Specific, there has never been too much detail.

General and Specific are the endpoints on a continuum of behavior: A great many people are not fully one or the other. Your prospects will require varying levels of detail. It is important to match that level when making your presentation because that is the precise amount of detail they want from you. This category of the Human Operating System determines the style of language that will establish rapport between the two of you, whether it is spare or full of details.

In a selling situation, listen to the customer's responses to any of your questions. If you do not have a clear moving picture of what was said, then the customer is someone who sorts information more generally. As the customer gives more detail, they sort more specifically.

We recall a customer telling about a "problem" that he and his wife had concerning investments:

Whenever the man wanted to invest in a particular product or piece of real estate, he would go home and basically tell his wife, "I have a great investment opportunity for us. It's a piece of property, and the returns will be excellent. We'll be able to get out of it in a few years and make some money."

Whenever he did this, he said that his wife would look at him very oddly and say, "What are you talking about? How can we put our money in something like that? Tell me more about it. What kind of investment is it? Where is it? How much money do we have to put in? What does the market research show?" She would barrage him with specific questions, until the customer said he would get pretty upset. With that kind of intense questioning, he thought his wife didn't trust his judgment. But it actually was nothing that serious. The fact was that he took in information in big chunks, and his wife wanted information in lots of small pieces. Of course, at that point we knew that we should be more general in our presentation. However, if we were selling to his wife, we would be ready to give plenty of details.

The Question for Process Scope

The following request reveals your Process Scope. Please answer it on a sheet of paper or into a tape recorder.

TELL ME ABOUT ONE OF YOUR FAVORITE
working experiences.
(Movies or books will also do as a context.)
(The request must be answered with a one-time event.)

How to Interpret What You Hear

Modifiers are the first clue in identifying these patterns. A Specific fills his or her speech with adjectives and adverbs. When answering your inquiry about a favorite experience, count the modifiers: A total Specific will often use two or more per sentence. This person will also give concrete examples: "I saw a great film last Tuesday, the

16th. We always go to the early show because it's only two-fifty then. They were showing a double feature of *Cool Hand Luke* and *The Verdict*. I just love Paul Newman's blue eyes and the way he talks so soft and slow." That would be just the beginning, for a Specific will happily tell you the entire cast as well as the plot of both movies. If they tell it to you in sequence, then you will have a Procedures as well as Specific. Be sure to give these people plenty of time because they won't feel complete if they don't get to tell the whole story from beginning to end.

The General person will answer the movie question simply. "I like going to movies." Getting details requires interrogation: asking specific questions, and sometimes asking them more than once.

Dialogue A

Julie: Gene, we talked about what you want in an automobile, and I believe I can help you. I am wondering, **COULD YOU TELL ME ABOUT THE LAST FAVORABLE EXPERIENCE** you had when buying a car?

Gene: This is the first car I ever bought.

Julie: I see. I am curious, **WHAT WAS THE LAST ITEM YOU PURCHASED** that gave you the same criteria you are looking for in an automobile ... you know, quality, dependability?

Gene: Well, I have been wanting an electric razor for some time and I thought why not, I have been cutting myself with razor blades too long. So just the other day, Tuesday to be exact, I went shopping for an electric razor. I got up at 7:00 A.M. and didn't shave because I wanted to try each razor until I found one that did a good job. You know, a smooth cut without pain. I had breakfast close to the mall and then immediately started to shop when the stores opened at 9:00 A.M. I went to three stores before I found the right razor. It was a Remington with all the bells and whistles. I shaved what was left after six trial shaves with other razors and made the decision on the spot. You know when you have found the right thing. Well. . . .

Obviously, Gene thrives on detail. A key to deciding whether someone is Specific is whether you can get a clear understanding of what they are talking about. Is it like a movie, or more like snapshots? The key is the amount of detail: Gene averages more than one per sentence in this paragraph, and that would be the level of specificity he would feel most comfortable with when Julie responds. (Gene also exhibits a Procedures pattern because of the way he sequences the story. And he also demonstrates the speech pattern of an Internal in the last line.)

Dialogue B

Julie: I am curious, Tom, **WHAT WAS THE LAST ITEM YOU PURCHASED** that gave you the same criteria you are looking for in an automobile...you know, quality, dependability?

Tom: I bought an electric razor last week. It was something I had wanted for quite some time.

Tom only uses two modifiers, "electric" and "last," which in this context are hardly enlightening details. His sequence is reversed: He tells us his behavior and then what motivated it.

The answers you get from your clients may not be so pronounced; however, they will be filled with clues. In evaluating their answers, listen for modifiers and sequences. Specific dates or times indicate both detail and sequence, strong evidence of a Specific speech pattern.

Abstract examples and generalities turn up in the typically brief answers of a General pattern. They will ignore your request for a specific event and answer with a vague range of behaviors—"I like going to movies," "I liked working in the benefits department," "I really enjoy fishing in the summer." They tend to summarize where a Specific will elaborate.

How Process Scope Affects the Sales Cycle

As with the other patterns, the key to using Process Scope is matching your prospect's language pattern in your own speech, which creates rapport. A person who feels comfortable with the big picture will feel frustrated and oppressed by too many particulars. When presenting your information to a General, concentrate on the overall direction and don't spend a lot of time on the smaller details. If you do, they will quickly get bored, trance out, and pay no attention to your presentation. Here's how you might deal with a General:

> Tom, as you drive this car, you may notice the overall ride and the feel of solid construction along with smoothness. Having a car that is stylish and dependable along

with the other benefits is something that you said you wanted, isn't it?

When selling to a Specific, put your information into small chunks and concentrate on the details. Specifics do not concern themselves with the outcome so much as with the steps involved. Rather than give them a short summary of what your product will do, break it down into a series of how it will benefit them. They feel cheated by generalities. If you fail to give them information in the small chunks with which they are comfortable, they will be frustrated and seek out other sources. In order to decide, they need specifics, otherwise they will refuse to decide on grounds of insufficient data. It's your job to see that they have that information.

> Tom, as you drive this car you may notice how solid it feels because of the extra suspension and oversized motor mounts that are standard on this car only, and with that added advantage you might also notice how smooth it feels. The tires are a new design with a split wedge for greater safety on slick surfaces and more cushion on bumpy roads. The details of this car, like the rolled-edge in the seats that give them extra strength, add to the style. Notice the advanced gauges, like a Boeing 707, and how easy they are to read as you are driving. At night they really add to your ability to see without distracting you from the road.

If you cannot find a way to work this question into your initial inquiries with a customer, you can still identify the pattern by listening closely to their answers to the other questions. A General will always answer in generalities and with abstract examples. Specifics will respond in detailed, sequenced, and concrete examples. The more detail your customer gives you, the more he or she will want from you. When you match that level of detail, they will feel synchronized with you.

For a few days, practice only this question with your friends and colleagues. It will not take you long to feel comfortable identifying this speech pattern in others. Once you know what pattern they are, match them in their level of detail and watch how they respond. There are many things—body language, voice tone and inflection, willingness to answer—that will tell you whether you are in rapport with someone. Once you have rapport, deliberately mismatch them and observe the response. You will quickly discover the powerful effects of Process Scope in creating effective communication.

What Is Your Process Scope?

How did you answer the question? Did you tell a story in a sequence? Would someone reading or hearing your answer know the details of your experience? Or would they be lost, knowing only the overall direction? How big were the chunks of information you answered with? Did you give abstract examples or concrete ones?

When you are clear about your pattern, turn to pages 163–164 and mark that box in your HOS Profile Chart.

Practice Makes Perfect

The patterns for Process Scope are simple to decipher: Does the person answer with a story full of details, or do they leave you with just the barest understanding of their situation? Answers appear on pages 114–117.

Example 1

Susan: Bill, I know you've bought equipment like this before, and I'm very happy you're interested in our equipment. Could you tell me about your experience with your other vendor?

Bill: You know, when we started out with our first big order about seven years ago, I would never have guessed that some day I would be big enough to go directly to the manufacturer. But we've grown so fast—we've increased our sales by more than twelve percent each of the last five years. In that time, we've doubled our sales force, and the distributors, like Henry's company— Henry was our old rep—just couldn't give us the kind of delivery we needed. We've refined our procedures around here till we pretty much run on next-day delivery. Plus the shipping costs were mounting because their distribution center was near Denver. Shipping had gone from one to three percent of cost, and we just couldn't see how it was ever going to come down. It was just a matter of getting too big, I guess.

Example 2

Tory: Heather, would you tell me about the last movie you saw that you liked?

Heather: Oh, I loved that movie with Laura What's Her Name. You know the one, it was a romantic comedy. It was out last year sometime. They were so cute together, but I'd never seen him in anything. It was just one of those real sweet movies.

Example 3

John: Carmen, you sound excited about going on vacation. Could you tell me about the last time you had fun on a vacation?

Carmen: Now that would be easy. Bob and I took a Caribbean cruise three years ago, and it was to die for. We made seven ports-of-call in eight days. No phones, fabulous food. Just everything you could possibly want. More food than an army could eat. Brenda Banks, the famous singer, did two shows. Bob drove golf balls off the bow. I got a massage every day. We had the most romantic night in St. Martin, and then Bob lost $150 at the casino in San Juan. Everything was just perfect, and it didn't cost but $760 each, plus the airfare. It was a bargain.

Example 4

Mason: We've been trying for an hour to decide where we're going to go eat. Why don't you tell me about your favorite eating experience and that will help me think up some alternatives.

Sylvia: Let's see, the one that really sticks out goes back a long way. I was dating a guy who later became my first husband. I think it was probably our first date, and he took me to this place on the harbor. It was like a dive, I thought, but inside it was really charming—Mediterranean, candles in pot-bellied Ruffino bottles, that kind of thing. All seafood menu, incredible selection. I had never had crab, and we shared Alaska king crab legs. And he was being so sweet. I fell in love that night. We used to go there for anniversaries.

Reviewing further is essential to learning how to distinguish the patterns in Process Scope. We suggest you ask this question, in a variety of contexts, of anyone who will let you record their answer on tape. At home, play their answers. It will take very few examples for you to begin to see the various levels of detail people use. Some pour it on, others sprinkle it, and still others dole out specifics as if they were gold nuggets.

Answers to the Review

Example 1

Bill: You know, when we started out with our first big order about SEVEN YEARS ago, I would never have guessed that some day I would be big enough to go directly to the manufacturer. But we've grown so fast—we've INCREASED OUR SALES BY MORE THAN TWELVE PERCENT EACH OF THE LAST FIVE YEARS. In that time we've DOUBLED OUR SALES FORCE, and the distributors, like Henry's company—HENRY WAS OUR OLD REP—just couldn't give us the kind of delivery we needed. We've refined our procedures around here till we pretty much run on NEXT-DAY DELIVERY. Plus the shipping costs were mounting because their DISTRIBUTION CENTER WAS NEAR DENVER. SHIPPING HAD GONE FROM ONE TO THREE PERCENT OF COST, and we just couldn't see how it was ever going to come down. It was just a matter of us getting too big, I guess.

Bill is a Specific; he feels comfortable with a high level of numbers and facts. One specific per sentence would suit him just fine.

Example 2

Heather: Oh, I loved that movie with Laura What's Her Name. You know the one, it was a romantic comedy. It was out last year sometime. They were so cute together, but I'd never seen him in anything. It was just one of those real sweet movies.

Heather is a General. She edits out details and feels comfortable with an overall picture.

Example 3

Carmen: Now that would be easy. BOB AND I TOOK A CARIBBEAN CRUISE THREE YEARS AGO, and it was to die for. We made SEVEN PORTS-OF-CALL IN EIGHT DAYS. No phones, fabulous food. Just everything you could possibly want. MORE FOOD THAN AN ARMY COULD EAT. BRENDA BANKS, THE FAMOUS SINGER, DID TWO SHOWS. BOB DROVE GOLF BALLS OFF THE BOW. I GOT A MASSAGE EVERY DAY. WE HAD THE MOST ROMANTIC NIGHT IN ST. MARTIN, AND THEN BOB LOST $150 AT THE CASINO IN SAN JUAN. Everything was just perfect, and it didn't cost but $760 EACH PLUS THE AIRFARE. It was a bargain.

Carmen is definitely a Specific.

Example 4

Sylvia: Let's see, the one that really sticks out goes back a long way. I was dating a guy WHO LATER BECAME MY FIRST HUSBAND. He took me to this place on the harbor. It was a dive, I thought, but inside it was really charming—MEDITERRANEAN CANDLES IN POT-BELLIED RUFFINO BOTTLES, that kind of thing. They had the most incredible selection of seafood. I had

never had crab, and we shared
ALASKA KING CRAB LEGS. And he
was being so sweet. I fell in love that
night. We used to go there for anniversaries.

Sylvia is more General than Specific. She does throw
in a few details, about one every other sentence, but she
does not crave them. She will be most comfortable with a
moderate level of detail.

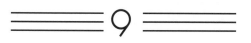

CLIENT DISAGREEMENT *CAN* CLOSE THE SALE

When you look at individual examples of things, do you compare them, that is, note how they are the same, or do you contrast them, by which we mean concentrate on how they are different? Comparing and contrasting—that is how we learn. There is no other way short of divine revelation. Whether you distinguish through similarities or differences defines your "Process Relationship."

Process Relationship

Four patterns make up this category: Same, Same/ Difference, Difference, and Difference/Same. These patterns are potent factors in rapport building and information transfer. Think of them as processing strategies. It is crucial that you know a person's processing strategy if you want to influence this person, such as getting him or her to understand how good your product is. When you match their strategy, you have the edge in getting them to understand what you tell them.

Same

The Same individual likes the world to stay calm and regular. This person thrives on routine and does not seek new challenges or experiment with new approaches to work. In

Category	*Question*
Motivating Language	For you, what is important about *selling*?
Motivating Direction	What do you want *from selling?* What will having *that* really do for you?
Motivating Source	How do you know *that you've done a good job*?
Process Approach	Why did you choose *to be a salesman/woman*?
Decision Strategy	How do you know that *your supplier/accountant/lawyer* is good *at their job*?
Convincer Strategy	How many times do they have to demonstrate this (*that they are good at their job*) before you are convinced?
Process Scope	Tell me about one of your favorite *working experiences.*
Process Relationship	What is the relationship between *what you are doing this year on your job and what you did last year on your job*?

fact, if too much change is introduced in a meeting, for instance, he or she will likely build stress and break rapport. Same people typically stay with one product or service for long periods of time, as long as the Sameness matches their criteria. They strive for normalcy. These people are often considered inflexible because they simply will not broach change. Change, any change, distresses them, and they adapt to it poorly.

Same/Difference

A person with this pattern appreciates regularity and normalcy, and at the same time requires variety. If work does not provide it, this person will initiate it, seeking out new but related activities. He or she enjoys finding new ways of doing things and improving on routines, adapts well to change, and will follow through on long-term projects. When speaking with a Same/Difference person, it is important to balance sameness with a new approach.

Difference and Difference/Same

People with these patterns thrive on change. In fact, to be happy, they must have new and different activities or leading-edge products or new and different approaches to service. They do not tolerate routines and will force change in order to satisfy this pattern. If they cannot make that happen, they will change suppliers. They are sometimes experienced as people who disagree a lot with the opinions of other people.

The Question for Process Relationship

The following question elicits responses that reveal a person's Process Relationship. Please answer it on a sheet of paper or into a tape recorder.

WHAT IS THE RELATIONSHIP BETWEEN
what you are doing this year on your job and what you did last year on your job?

How to Interpret What You Hear

Same and Difference patterns answer the relationship question with opposite responses. You only need to listen for whether they tell you how things are the same or how they are different.

Dialogue A

Sue: Bill, we have not had an opportunity to talk about your business, and I know that when I learn more about how you developed and grew your company, I will be able to see how my services will be more useful to you. I am curious about **THE RELATIONSHIP BETWEEN WHAT YOUR BUSINESS WAS LIKE LAST YEAR AND WHAT YOU ARE DOING THIS YEAR.**

Bill: I don't know how that can help you, but I can tell you that it is totally different. If you stay on the same track, you fall into a rut. This year we are focusing on the international market almost exclusively. Last year we concentrated on building our domestic network.

Dialogue B

Sue: Bob, we have not had an opportunity to talk about your business, and I know that when I learn more about how you developed and grew your company, I will be able to see how my services will be more useful to you. I am curious about **THE RELATIONSHIP BETWEEN WHAT YOUR BUSINESS WAS LIKE LAST YEAR AND WHAT YOU ARE DOING THIS YEAR.**

Bob: Sue, that is a good question. When I really think about it, I believe that the business is basically the same. We don't change things when they are working.

Dialogue C

Sue: Barney, we have not had an opportunity to talk about your business, and I know that when I learn more about how you developed and grew your company, I will be able to see how my services will be more useful to you. I am curious about **THE RELATIONSHIP BETWEEN WHAT YOUR BUSINESS WAS LIKE LAST YEAR AND WHAT YOU ARE DOING THIS YEAR.**

Barney: I'd have to say it's pretty much the same, only better. You know, you're hopefully always improving. It's the same business, the same customers and deadlines, but we seem to handle them with more grace, and we definitely finesse better at what we don't know.

Dialogue D

Sue: Bailey, we have not had an opportunity to talk about your business, and I know that when I learn more about how you developed and grew your company, I will be able to see how my services will be more useful to you. I am curious about **THE RELATIONSHIP BETWEEN WHAT YOUR BUSINESS WAS LIKE LAST YEAR AND WHAT YOU ARE DOING THIS YEAR.**

Bailey: When I think about all the changes, well, it's almost not the same business: new personnel, new machines, new customers, but the same products and the same suppliers. So, you know, it all balances out.

People almost always answer the relationship question with patterns this clear. You can easily see that Bill in Dialogue A is the Difference pattern. By questioning what good that does her, he even "differences" the reason for the question. Then, he tells Sue that his business is "totally different," they aren't even dealing with the same market. But you are probably asking yourself, "What if the business really has changed? How else could Bill answer then?"

The actual state or rate of change doesn't matter in identifying the pattern, because if Bill were a Same, he would have found something that was the same to answer with: We're making the same product, we're still at the same address, we have the same employees. There would be many things that hadn't changed, and a Same person would focus on those.

On the other hand, a Difference person will find how things are different because that is what *relationship* means to them.

In Dialogue B, Bob is a Same: He sees how this year is the same as last year and makes no distinction between the two. Were there really no differences worth mentioning? Unlikely, but Bob does not concentrate on that. Sue asked for the relationship, and that is what *relationship* means to him, how things are the same.

In Dialogue C, Barney tells Sue how things are the same and then adds how they're different. Whenever you hear comparative words like "more," "better," and "improve," that is the speech pattern of Same/Difference. They see things in terms of evolution and will emphasize gradual improvements rather than radical changes. They learn by comparing things first and then contrasting them.

In Dialogue D, Bailey tells Sue how this year is different, but then he adds how it is the same, so he is a Difference/Same. This speech pattern contrasts first and then compares.

Whenever you hear words like "although," "but," and "except," you are dealing with one of the Split patterns. Another very strong clue for identifying any one of the patterns is how long a person has been in his or her job. If they've been there more than two years, it is unlikely that they are either of the Difference patterns. If they've been in the same job (not just with the same company) more than ten years, it's likely they are a Same. However, before assuming their pattern from that evidence, ask the relationship question just to make sure. You never know about companies, many internal changes can occur. They could have worked at the same place ten years and had thirty different projects. Or they could have changed jobs often because their responsibilities kept changing and that made them unhappy.

If you feel as if you are not getting a clear answer to your question, follow up their answer by asking "The relationship then is . . . ?" and let them fill in the blank. People will almost always say "the same," "different," or use some comparative phrase with "better," "less," or "more."

How Process Relationship Affects the Sales Cycle

Your prospects' Process Relationship is a crucial component of their information-gathering process. Knowing that process allows you to fit your information into it, which dramatically increases the likelihood that they will be able to take in what you have to say.

For example, a person who learns by calibrating how things are different will not respond to explanations of how your product is like something else he or she is already using. For this person, it is vital that you distinguish yourself immediately if you want to make an impact. Observe the deliberate "difference-ing" in this response:

> Bill, our services provide our customers a way to expand and profit in these tough economic times because of the NEW TECHNIQUES we use. I'm NOT SURE THESE ARE SERVICES YOU CAN USE at this time in your business growth. A company has to be positioned just right for the change.

On the other hand, emphasizing differences with a Same assures communication failure and a missed sale. If you want these potential customers to grasp your presentation, explain how your product is the same as what they are using and then distinguish yourself by "same-ing" their criteria. Here's an example of how to touch them:

> Our services have proven to be a way for our customers to MAINTAIN their business in these tough economic times. Our TIME-PROVEN TECH-NIQUES continue to support customers such as yourself because they are tried and TESTED OVER

TIME AND SIMILAR TO OTHER SUCCESSFUL APPROACHES.

Our experience has shown that the majority of decision-makers you deal with are Same/Difference people. Communicating effectively with them is simply a matter of same-ing their learning strategy: explain how you are the same as what they are using, only better. They feel comfortable with comparative words like "more," "better," "best," and "improved."

Concerning the Difference/Same pattern, you treat them essentially the same as a Difference, emphasizing the differences. This is the rarest strategy of the four. Both types of Difference individuals are moved by phrases like "different," "changed," "unique," "new," and "revolutionary."

During one of Marvin's training programs, a participant named Bill stated that what Marvin was saying was totally ridiculous. Bill argued that he had been in the selling business for over twenty-five years and really knew how to sell. This interruption was made during a presentation on how to build rapport. Marvin knew that the man did not have anything personal against him as the trainer, his brain was only sorting for differences. As Marvin approached this fellow, he aligned with him by repeating his statement that Bill knew how to sell because he'd been at it for twenty-five years, and then said, "You may not believe this, Bill, but this information could be useful for some of these people with less experience."

With that, Marvin turned and restarted his program. However, in a few moments, Bill interrupted again by saying quite loudly, "Wait a minute. Hold it, just wait one minute." Marvin expected some more conversation regarding mismatching, but this time Bill said, "You know, that is exactly what I do, what you're saying is exactly what

I do. I was just thinking back on the sales calls I make and I do that unconsciously." Miracle of miracles, Marvin got a person with a Difference pattern to match him.

This is how Marvin did it: Initially he mismatched his statement to Bill by saying, "Bill, you won't believe this. . . ." Of course, Bill's brain mismatched that, that is, inside himself, he said, "I will believe this." That simple prologue released his ability to evaluate and analyze what Marvin was saying so he could see how it really did fit into the process of building relationships. Put even more simply, he mismatched not believing and believing. People with Difference patterns will really test you, until you realize how they process relationships. Before you get upset with them, just realize that, trying as it may be, they learn by contrasting things.

Alternative Questions

WHAT IS THE RELATIONSHIP BETWEEN *the investments you made last year and the ones you're making this year?*

WHAT IS THE RELATIONSHIP BETWEEN *your business activity last year and your approach to business this year?*

(ALWAYS ask for "the relationship," NOT for "the difference.")

What is Your Process Relationship?

Evaluate your own answer to this question and decide which pattern best identifies your learning strategy. Did you cite how things are the same, or did you emphasize how they are different? Perhaps they were better? After you have identified yourself, mark the appropriate box in the HOS Profile Chart on pages 163–164.

Practice Makes Perfect

The question you must answer to identify Process Relationship is this, does the person compare or contrast? Do they look for differences or similarities? Answers appear on pages 131–132.

Example 1

> *Kevin:* Using a firm such as ours can be very rewarding when introducing a new manufacturing process. We've discussed the way we operate and the development of your marketing campaign over the phone. It would help me if I knew more about the relationship between the products you're selling this year and those you sold last year.

> *Jennifer:* This year we are selling more color and updated design. It's much more contemporary.

Example 2

> *Bryan:* Could you explain to me the relationship between what you're marketing this year and last year's product line?

> *Kathryn:* Basically it's the same product. You know, a winner is a winner. It's impor-

tant that people have learned to trust us long-term. That's more valuable than a million dollars a year in advertising.

Example 3

Jason: What is the relationship between what you are doing this year on your job and what you did last year?

Carl: I guess the biggest difference is the technology, and the numbers, too. But overall, it's the same business, same customers. The paperwork is different, computerized, but we're still trying to accomplish the same things day-to-day, keep the overhead monster at bay.

Example 4

Ronald: Your company has been so successful over the years. It's really amazing. It just makes me wonder, what is the relationship between what you're doing this year and what you were doing last year?

Louise: It seems to me that it changes pretty dramatically from year to year. I mean there's so much turnover in employees and suppliers and new accounts. But it can't be all that different because, I mean, we're still selling the same products, or the same kind anyway, to the same kinds of businesses.

Reviewing further is essential to learning how to distinguish the patterns in Process Relationship. We suggest you ask this question, in a variety of contexts, of anyone who will let you record their answer on tape. At home, play their responses. You will quickly be able to distinguish whether someone "sames" or "differences," whether they compare or contrast.

Answers to the Review

Example 1

> *Jennifer:*   This year we are selling MORE color and updated design. It's MUCH MORE contemporary.

Jennifer is Difference; "more" reflects comparison.

Example 2

> *Kathryn:*   Basically it's the same product. You know, a winner is a winner. It's important that people have learned to trust us long-term. That's more valuable than a million dollars a year in advertising.

Kathryn is a Same.

Example 3

> *Carl:*   I guess the biggest DIFFERENCE is the technology, and the numbers, too. But overall, I do the SAME THING, DEAL WITH THE SAME CUSTOMERS. The paperwork is DIFFERENT, for sure,

computerized, but I try to accomplish the SAME THINGS DAY-TO-DAY: keep the overhead monster at bay.

Carl is Difference/Same.

Example 4

Louise: It seems to me that it CHANGES PRETTY DRAMATICALLY FROM YEAR TO YEAR. I mean there's SO MUCH TURNOVER in employees and suppliers and NEW ACCOUNTS. But it can't be all that different because, I mean, we're STILL SELL-ING THE SAME PRODUCTS, OR THE SAME KIND ANYWAY, TO THE SAME KINDS OF BUSINESSES.

Louise is also Difference/Same.

Review of Chapters 8 & 9

Later that afternoon, Huggins and Miller come back together for a brief discussion. Can you ferret out Mr. Miller's Process Scope and his Process Relationship?

Huggins:	We had a full day, and I have gathered enough information to identify the scope of my proposal.
Miller:	Before you get into the detail, tell me what you think of the manager.
Huggins:	I'll be happy to do that, but could you tell me about one of your favorite working experiences.
Miller:	Oh, that would be hard to do. I love this job.
Huggins:	Then you must have lots of stories. Tell me one of them.
Miller:	Well, I guess the best time I remember was when we got the Dunston contract. It took a helluva long time, a year and a few days, and then one of our key subcontractors went belly up. I mean we

really had to get our act together to perform. We had guys working up here round the clock for about a week. It was a mess, but we pulled it off.

Huggins: Sounds like one of those events that really brings a group of people together.

Miller: Yeah, I guess it was our trial by fire, but anyway, what about that manager?

Huggins: I believe that he has the capability to do the job. He is a bit overwhelmed because of the volume of input and the limited resources he has for dealing with the information explosion. Conceptually, he picks up pretty quickly.

Miller: OK, that's all I was needing. Can you give me a bottom line on what you think we need? I don't have time now to get into the nitty-gritty.

Huggins: May I ask you a question before I get started? It will help me understand more about your present system failure.

Miller: Sure.

Huggins: What is the relationship between the distributor sales this year and the distributor sales last year?

Miller: What is the relationship? Well, it is similar from the standpoint of distributor base, but it has grown substantially in volume. The changes were slow in coming, that's why we have been caught without a way to respond. Now we are in a crisis mode. If we don't get a handle on the situation quickly, we are going to have a loss in profit, and that's something I don't want.

Huggins: Good, that helps me a lot. I believe that we can get a handle on the situation pretty fast. Based on what I saw today and your present capabilities in the department, I will be able to put a system together that will be similar in many ways to your present function, and with some additional equipment and software you will be on top of your accounts within a short period of time. Your problems are not gigantic now, and I would suggest that timing is very important. I will put together a proposal tomorrow and deliver it by four o'clock. I will also include references and letters from past customers. Is there anything else you will need before making a decision?

Miller: That will work for me. If things check out, I don't think I'll be talking to anyone else.

Huggins: I'll talk with you tomorrow afternoon. Should I bring some apple pastry?

Answers to the Review

Process Scope

Mr. Miller is a mixed pattern, more General than Specific. He uses very little detail and few modifiers in his answer.

Process Relationship

He is Same/Difference. He sees similarities and then differences.

═══ 10 ═══

Putting It All Together:
The Most Important Chapter of All

Clearly, the secret to success with learning this material is to practice, practice, practice. There is nothing magical about any of this information, it is just a matter of learning. With that in mind, we have added three complete interviews that use all the questions. Read through these and put down your evaluations of each of the patterns, then look at the answers at the end and check out how you did.

If you really want to learn these techniques, interviewing people on tape and then listening to their answers until you can clearly identify the patterns will make a quantum difference in your understanding. Good luck.

The table containing the HOS Profile questions appears on the next page for your review.

Category	*Question*
Motivating Language	For you, what is important about *selling*?
Motivating Direction	What do you want *from selling?* What will having *that* really do for you?
Motivating Source	How do you know *that you've done a good job*?
Process Approach	Why did you choose *to be a salesman/woman*?
Decision Strategy	How do you know that *your supplier/accountant/lawyer* is good *at their job*?
Convincer Strategy	How many times do they have to demonstrate this (*that they are good at their job*) before you are convinced?
Process Scope	Tell me about one of your favorite *working experiences.*
Process Relationship	What is the relationship between *what you are doing this year on your job and what you did last year on your job*?

Sales Meeting With Potential Customer/Client

Salesperson: Fran Cummings
Customer: Bob Adams

1 Fran:	Good morning, Mr. Adams.
2 Bob:	Yes!
3a Fran: *b* *c* *d* *e* *f* *g* *h*	Thank you for arranging your time to meet with me. As we discussed on the telephone last week, I represent Office Supply Discounts. My purpose is to save you money and time when your company buys supplies. Those are some of the things you mentioned you wanted, aren't they?
4 Bob:	Yes.
5a Fran: *b* *c* *d* *e* *f*	I would like to ask you a few questions that will help me be as brief as possible. Mr. Adams, you have used other suppliers in the past and I am wondering what is really important for you in the supplier you use?
6a Bob: *b* *c*	I want fast service, good prices, and quality in the products I buy, especially equipment.
7a Fran: *b*	Mr. Adams, have you had some problems with past equipment purchases?
8a Bob: *b*	Well, the last copier I bought was supposed to save my people time and

e	ended up costing me time because it was
f	complicated and broke down a lot.

9a Fran:	I can sure appreciate how frustrating it is
b	to spend good money and not receive
c	what you thought you were going to get.
d	I have a number of customers who, prior
e	to going with us, had similar experiences.
f	Mr. Adams, may I ask you what else
g	would having a supplier that gave you
h	fast service, good prices, and quality
i	products really do for you?

10a Bob:	Do for me? Well, I wouldn't have to
b	worry about wasting time and wasting
c	money.

11a Fran:	Absolutely, that's what my customers
b	tell me often about our service. In the
c	past, when going with other service
d	providers, how did you know you
e	made a good decision at the time you
f	made it?

12a Bob:	At the time, I just felt the people could
b	perform. You never really know for sure,
c	but I believe you have to go with your
d	gut.

13a Fran:	That is true, you never really know on the
b	front end. Mr. Adams, it would be useful
c	for me to know how you recognize that
d	someone is good at their job.

14a Bob:	That's hard to know, but I figure if they
b	can put it in layman's terms, they prob-
c	ably know what's going on.

15a Fran:
b
c

How many times would a supplier have to perform before you were really convinced that they could do a good job?

16a Bob:
b

Every time. People change and so do the circumstances.

17a Fran:
b
c
d
e
f
g

That's what is important about my job, I have to make sure that we are giving our customers fast, inexpensive, and quality service all the time. You mentioned that you bought a copier recently. Why did you choose that particular model?

18a Bob:
b
c

It gave me what I wanted, I thought. Good copies, fast reproduction, and overall quality.

19a Fran:
b
c
d
e
f
g

You have been in business, as I understand, for a number of years. From the standpoint of us providing the kind of service you need, what is the relationship between what you are doing this year and what you were doing last year?

20a Bob:
b
c
d
e

Our business is changing all the time. What we are doing now is different in many ways, although we have maintained a similar product line and customer base.

21a Fran:
b
c
d

Things are changing all the time, and you do have to be alert for new ways to stay ahead of the competition. Mr. Adams, my customers have found it

e	very helpful, before we started han-
f	dling their supplies, to analyze past
g	purchases in order to confirm that we
h	can provide a less expensive service
i	and meet your timing requirements. I
j	can do this very quickly, it's up to
k	you, and without the need for you to
l	get involved in the detail. Who in
m	your organization could get the
n	invoices for the past quarter?

22a Bob:	Janice Fellows, our office manager,
b	can handle that.

23a Fran:	Great. I can take care of that right now
b	and then I can give you the summary
c	of my findings. I want to be sure that
d	when I say we can give you better
e	prices and fast service with quality
f	products, I know that is the case. There
g	would be no reason to change suppli-
h	ers if you didn't receive the benefit of
i	not wasting time and money.

What is Bob Adams's HOS Profile?

His Criteria? _____

Moving Toward/Away From? _____

Internal/External? _____

Options/Procedures? _____

Automatic/Consistent/Examples/Time? _____

Difference/Same? _____

General/Specific? _____

Visual/Auditory/Feelings? _____

Correct Answers

Motivating Language: Fast Service, Good Prices, Quality

Bob lists his criteria in lines 6a-b.

Motivating Direction: Away-From

In paragraph 9g-i, Fran asks the Motivating Direction question using Bob's criteria from the first question, ". . . what else would having a supplier that gave you fast service, good prices, and quality products really do for you?" Bob answers succinctly in paragraph 10a-c: "I wouldn't have to worry about wasting time and money." Bob is Away-From because he identifies a problem ("worry about wasting time and wasting money"), rather than naming something he wants to gain or achieve.

Motivating Source: Internal

Fran asks Bob the Motivating Source question in 11d-f. Bob answers in paragraph 12a-d. It is clear that Bob sorts internally because he refers to no one else in his answer.

Process Approach: Options

Fran asks the Process Approach question in paragraph 17f-g, "Why did you choose that particular model?" Bob answers in paragraph 18a-c. His answer is pure Options because it consists of nothing but criteria, no story, no sequence. He answers a "why" question, not a "how" question, which would be the mark of a Procedures pattern: "Good copies, faster reproduction, and overall quality."

Convincer Strategy: Consistent

Fran asks the Convincer Strategy question in 15a-c, and Bob answers in paragraph 16. Bob is someone who cuts no slack; people have to perform "every time" for him. Bob is never sure that you can do the job. He also gives us a hint in his answer to the Motivating Source question in paragraph 12b-c when he says, "You never really know for sure. . . ."

Process Relationship: More Difference Than Same

Fran asks the Process Relationship question in 19d-g. Bob answers in 20a-e. He begins by discussing differences ("changing all the time," "now is different"), and then talks about similarities ("similar product line and customer base").

Process Scope: General

First of all, notice that Bob never gets very specific in any of his answers. He gives more general answers so that Fran really does not have all the information she needs. If you go through and count the details he relates, you will find very few. When someone gives general answers and is not giving you every item that you could possibly want to know, they are sorting more General.

Decision Strategy: Auditory

Fran asks the Decision Strategy question in paragraph 13b-e. Bob answers in paragraph 14, and the key in his answer is "if they can put it in layman's terms"— clearly this is a phrase that reflects someone who is listening for information.

Telephone Sales Call

Salesperson: Al
Customer: Jane

1 Al:		Good afternoon.
2 Jane:		Good afternoon, what can I do for you?
3a Al: *b* *c*		Your receptionist told me that you are responsible for the credit department with your company. Is that correct?
4a Jane: *b* *c* *d* *e*		That's right, I handle all credit and collection for the company on a national basis. I do have three regional people reporting to me, but the bottom line is that I am responsible.
5a Al: *b* *c*		You must be quite busy with all that responsibility and the piles of detail it takes to be on top of all your customers.
6a Jane: *b* *c* *d*		Yes, it can be very detailed and time consuming. I didn't get out of here until 8:00 P.M. last night. So, what can I do for you and who are you?
7a Al: *b* *c* *d* *e* *f* *g* *h*		My name is Al Fisher, and I represent a service that many of my clients find to be a real time-saver for them. I handle filing and tracking of bonds and liens on credit risk customers. If my research is correct, you deal with a lot of small "mom and pop" operations and contractors. Is that correct?

8a Jane:
b
c
d
e
f
g

That's correct, Al, although I have been able to handle the lien and bonding side fairly well over the last few years. I wouldn't be interested in that kind of service unless you could really save me lots of time and could show me a track record of collecting the impossible.

9a Al:
b
c
d

Jane, that's exactly what we can do and more. What else would be important to you if you did use an outside service such as ours?

10a Jane:
b
c
d
e
f
g
h
i

Well, you would have to be available on a moment's notice and have connections around the country that could help us save time. Plus, you would have to have the ability to evaluate a customer's worth before we went through the process of establishing bonding needs. You would have to have a national network that could really help us.

11a Al:
b

If I could give you what you needed, what would that really do for you?

12a Jane:
b
c
d
e

It would give me the opportunity to get some of my projects off the ground and completed so our operation would be more effective. I doubt that you have that kind of service, Al.

13a Al:
b
c

Jane, many of our clients tell us that we can deliver results. Have you ever used outside services like ours?

14 Jane:

Yes, once in the past.

15a Al: I'm curious, Jane, when you hired the
   b   service, how did you know you made
   c   a good decision at the time you hired
   d   them?

16a Jane: I'm the kind of person that knows
   b   almost immediately whether it will
   c   work or not. What made you think
   d   you could help us?

17a Al: Before I answer that question, I'm
   b   curious to know how often some-
   c   one would have to do a good job
   d   for you in order for you to be con-
   e   vinced.

18a Jane: Well, Al, I'm a pretty tough person to
   b   convince. Just because you say it,
   c   doesn't mean it's true. Basically it
   d   would have to work for me every
   e   time.

19a Al: How would you really know if I did a
   b   good job?

20a Jane: I could see it in the bottom line and
   b   from the feedback I hear from the
   c   regional managers.

21a Al: Of course, the proof would have to be
   b   in the immediate results, and that
   c   decision would be strictly up to you. If
   d   you did decide that we could save you
   e   time, with a national availability that
   f   reacted to your immediate needs,
   g   what would be the first project we
   h   could work on?

22a Jane:
 b
 c

That's something we can talk about later. Tell me more about your service.

23a Al:
 b
 c
 d
 e
 f
 g

Jane, as a help for me to better understand the processes you're going through, and before I get into specifics, I am wondering what the relationship is between what you're doing this year and what you were doing last year.

24a Jane:
 b
 c
 d
 e
 f
 g
 h
 i
 j
 k
 l
 m
 n
 o
 p
 q
 r
 s
 t

If you mean the kind of work that I'm doing, it is exactly the same. The only change is the name of the customer and the amount of dollars. We approve credit on each purchase unless the customer has bought from us before and then we have an approved credit line. We update the credit work every quarter on customers, or if they haven't ordered in a quarter, we do a new financial on them.
Things change pretty fast with customers, and you can't believe their stories unless you have proof. If I make a wrong decision, it could cost my company big money. The sales people sure hate the way I hold up their orders when I do the financial work.

25a Al:
 b
 c
 d

Jane, if I could complete the financial work faster with precision, I'm sure that would be a major help for you. I'm wondering why you initially

e	chose the particular process that you
f	use.

26a Jane:	Oh yes, if you could complete the
b	financial work faster with precision,
c	that really would be a help to me.
d	Although I require the work to be
e	done according to specific procedures
f	that have been established here for
g	quite some time. I chose the structure
h	and process that we use many years
i	ago after working in a similar position
j	with another organization; I remem-
k	bered the process that they used and
l	how it could be improved to serve me
m	even better. When I came to this orga-
n	nization, I developed a similar process
o	with some of those additions to it and
p	it has worked very well, of course
q	except for the problem of time.

27a Al:	That's excellent, Jane. The first thing I
b	would like to do, if it is okay with you,
c	would be to visit to determine your
d	actual work flow. The second process
e	would be for me to fully and with spe-
f	cific detail explain how our service can
g	help you speed the process and do it
h	with precision on a national basis.
i	Third, we can examine how our fee
j	structure works and how that mea-
k	sures against your cost of doing busi-
l	ness. Fourth, we can identify in detail
m	the benefits you would receive, espe-
n	cially the help we could provide at
o	speeding up financial data gathering
p	within your procedure. Fifth, we can

q	conduct a trial project and when we
r	complete it successfully, we can cele-
s	brate our relationship with a lunch
t	before signing the agreement. So Jane,
u	what time this week would be conve-
v	nient for you to get started?

What is Jane's HOS Profile?

What Are Her Criteria? _____

Moving Toward/Away? _____

Internal/External? _____

Options/Procedures? _____

Automatic/Consistent/Examples/Time? _____

Difference/Same? _____

General/Specific? _____

Visual/Auditory/Feelings? _____

Correct Answers

Motivating Language: Save Lots of Time; Track Record of Collecting the Impossible; Available at a Moment's Notice; Connections Around the Country; Ability to Evaluate a Customer's Worth Before We Went Through the Process of Establishing Bonding Needs; National Network

Jane volunteers her criteria in paragraph 8e-g: "you could really save me lots of time and show me a track record of collecting the impossible." Al asks the Motivating Language question in paragraph 9b-d, and Jane adds more criteria in paragraph 10a-i, "You would have to be available at a moment's notice and have connections around the country that could help us save time." In addition, in that paragraph she talks about the ability to evaluate a customer's worth and have a national network. All of those statements and phrases are criteria answers.

Motivating Direction: Toward

Al asks the Motivating Direction question in paragraph 11. Jane answers it in 12a-d. Clearly she is looking for ways to satisfy her criteria and to expand her realm of possibilities by starting new projects; she even uses the word "opportunity." She is definitely not looking for what can go wrong so she can avoid it. She wants to achieve a goal.

Motivating Source: Internal

Al asks the Motivating Source question in paragraph 15a-d. Jane answers in paragraph 16a-b. Notice that Jane makes the determination through her own value system. She evaluates information in her own way by just knowing.

Process Approach: Procedures

In paragraph 25d-f, Al says, "I'm wondering why you initially chose the particular process that you use." In paragraph 26a-q, Jane answers the question by telling the story of how she chose the particular process.

Convincer Strategy: Consistent

In paragraph 17b-e, Al asks, "... how often someone would have to do a good job for you in order for you to be convinced." In paragraph 18a-e, you may notice that Jane said, "Well, Al, I'm a pretty tough person to convince. Just because you say it, doesn't mean it's true. Basically it would have to work for me every time."

Process Relationship: Same/Difference

Al asks the Process Relationship question in paragraph 23d-g. Jane answers in 24a-d by telling him that things are exactly the same, except for names and dollars. This answer indicates that she initially sorts for how things are the Same and then how they are Different.

Process Scope: Specific

The conversation used by Jane in most of the transaction gives Al quite a bit of information. For instance, in paragraph 6, she states, ". . . it can be very detailed and time consuming. I didn't get out of here until 8:00 PM last night." Basically she is providing more specific information to him, so he knows exactly and can probably paint the picture of what she is talking about. In paragraph 8 she gives more detail, this time about liens and bonding and exactly what she would be interested in. Notice that her conversation provides more information than the previous example with Mr. Adams.

Decision Strategy: Visual; Auditory

Al asks the Decision Strategy in paragraph 19. In paragraph 20a-c, Jane responds, "I could see it in the bottom line and from the feedback I hear from the regional managers." Obviously Jane sees a report (thus the bottom line) and she hears feedback.

Telephone Sales Call

Salesperson: Susan Schwartz
Customer: Alan Connors

1a Susan: *b* *c*	Good morning, Mr. Connors. My name is Susan Schwartz with Optimal Learning Technologies.
2a Connors: *b* *c*	Susan, I normally don't take direct calls like this, I'm wondering how you got my private number?
3a Susan: *b* *c* *d* *e* *f* *g* *h* *i* *j* *k*	Mr. Connors, I knew that you were the decision maker regarding training programs, so when I researched your company I basically asked for your private number. I know you've probably made these kinds of decisions before, and I'm wondering how you know that you've made a good decision when you hire a training organization.
4a Connors: *b* *c* *d* *e* *f* *g* *h* *i* *j* *k*	Well, I'm going to change the policies around here because I guess just about anybody can get through to me. Susan, I'm not interested in what you're selling, and when I've used training organizations before, I can tell immediately whether they can provide me with the kind of service that I want based on the feedback they give me regarding the outcome I'm seeking.

5a Susan:	Mr. Connors, I can appreciate what
b	you're saying, and I would hon-
c	estly be surprised if you were inter-
d	ested in what I was selling at this
e	point because I'm sure you need
f	quite a bit more information before
g	you can make a decision on any
h	type of service or product.
6 Connors:	Well, you have that right.
7a Susan:	Mr. Connors, it would be impos-
b	sible for me to sell you anything
c	over the telephone without
d	knowing whether what I have to
e	offer could even support or
f	enhance your particular needs.
g	So, it would be very useful if we
h	could talk personally to deter-
i	mine whether what I have
j	would be of any interest to you
k	at all. I'm wondering, Mr. Con-
l	nors, if you are in the middle of
m	a meeting now or can you spare
n	a few moments to help us make
o	that determination?
8a Connors:	Sure, go ahead. I have a few min-
b	utes.
9a Susan:	Mr. Connors, if you were to ever
b	use any outside training programs,
c	what would be important to you
d	about the type of resources we
e	could offer your organization or
f	your people that would be useful?

10a Connors: *b* *c* *d* *e* *f*	Well, the only thing that I'm interested in is whether the information I receive can be integrated by my people and can be applied specifically to what they are doing in order to increase sales.
11a Susan: *b* *c* *d* *e* *f* *g* *h* *i* *j* *k* *l* *m*	I'm glad that you mentioned that because integration of the material is what we specialize in, because if what we are saying can't be used, everybody is wasting time and money. Once this information is integrated, our clients tell us that they notice an immediate increase in sales as a result. I'm wondering, Mr. Connors, by having the kind of training that you want, what does that really do for you?
12a Connors: *b* *c* *d* *e* *f* *g* *h* *i* *j* *k* *l* *m*	Susan, what it does for me is help me get my company moving in a direction that's positive and gives the salespeople resources. Before we get going on any more specific questions, I'd like to hear from some of your clients before I even spend any time talking with you. I can make the decisions based on what people tell me, and I would also like to see a list of clients that you've worked with and the type of training that you've conducted.
13a Susan: *b*	I would be glad to supply you with that information yet I'm very

c d	curious, have you used outside training before?
14 Connors:	Yes, I have.
15a Susan: b c d	I'm wondering, when you made the decision to use an outside training organization, why did you choose the one you went with?
16a Connors: b c d e	Because after checking their references, I found that they could supply us with information that would help us make more money and make more sales.
17a Susan: b c d e f g h i	Well, that is the bottom line, Mr. Connors. Getting exactly what you want for the investment that you make. I'm curious, Mr. Connors, how often does the training company, such as the one you brought in, have to perform effectively for you before you're convinced that they can do a good job?
18a Connors: b c d e	Well, Susan, the fact is they have to do it every time. If they don't provide the information necessary for my people to be more successful, then they're out of here.
19a Susan: b c d e	I can definitely appreciate that. Mr. Connors, I am wondering, how would you know that someone was doing a good job for you and your people?

20a Connors: *b* *c* *d*	That's easy, you can hear the response of my people, and I could talk to each of them to be sure I was hearing right.
21a Susan: *b* *c* *d* *e* *f* *g* *h* *i* *j* *k*	What I would like to do is put together a list of organizations and companies which have experienced our training, along with the names of individuals and telephone numbers for you to contact directly. If it would be useful for you, I will also enclose a few letters of participants regarding the training and how they specifically received benefit from the information.
22a Connors: *b* *c* *d*	That would be fine. Just send them on over to me and I'll take a look at it and call some of the individuals.
23a Susan: *b* *c* *d* *e* *f* *g* *h* *i* *j* *k* *l* *m* *n* *o*	That's great, I will have this delivered to you by tomorrow morning, and if you don't mind, I would like to call you back to make sure that you received the information and that you have actually made contact with the references. Mr. Connors, there is just one more question I would like to ask you, and that is what is the relationship between the type of training you used last year and the training that you used the year before? This is an important factor for my planning purposes.

24a Connors: *b* *c* *d* *e* *f* *g* *h* *i* *j*	Relationship between the trainings? Well, Susan, there's no relationship between the two of them. I had different needs last year than I did the year before, just like I'll have this year. What difference would that make, seeing that we are going to create something that would fit what's important now.
25a Susan: *b* *c* *d* *e* *f* *g*	Mr. Connors, the fact is, it's now that counts, and what I would like to do is give you a call back on Friday of this week, or maybe it would be more useful for me to call you back on Monday as a follow-up.
26a Connors: *b* *c* *d*	Why don't you give me until next week. Susan, that will give me enough time to research the information that you sent over.
27a Susan: *b* *c* *d* *e* *f* *g* *h* *i* *j*	I appreciate your time on the phone, and I look forward to talking to you next week. I will be in town the balance of next week, and hopefully after our conversation we might be able to meet personally to discuss in depth the specific outcome that you would desire from any type of training.
28a Connors: *b*	That's fine, give me a call on Monday and I'll talk to you then.

What is Mr. Connors's HOS Profile?

His Criteria? _____

Moving Toward/Away? _____

Internal/External? _____

Options/Procedures? _____

Automatic/Consistent/Examples/Time? _____

Difference/Same? _____

General/Specific? _____

Visual, Auditory, Feelings? _____

Correct Answers

Motivating Language: Integrated by My People; Applied to What They Are Specifically Doing; Increase Sales

Additional Criteria: Help Us Make More Money and Make More Sales

Susan asks the Motivating Language question, "What would be important about the type of resources we could offer your organization?" in paragraph 9c-f. In paragraph 10c-f, Connors states his criteria; he states additional criteria in paragraph 16d-e.

Motivating Direction: Toward

Notice in paragraph 11j-m, Susan asks, "I'm wondering, Mr. Connors, by having the kind of training that you want, what does that really do for you?" In paragraph 12a-d, Connors states, "Susan, what it does for me is help me get my company moving in a direction that's positive and gives the salespeople resources." This identifies Connors as an individual that is talking about gaining something as opposed to losing something. The additional criteria he enumerates in paragraph 16d-e, ". . . information that would help us make more money and make more sales," is also a Toward language pattern. If he said that the reference checking or anything would keep him from having to worry about or losing something, that would be an Away-From motivation.

Motivating Source: Internal

Notice in paragraph 3i-k, Susan asks the question, ". . . how you know that you've made a good decision when you hire a training organization?" In paragraph 4f-k, Connors states, ". . . I can tell immediately whether they can provide me with the kind of service that I want based on the feedback they give me regarding the outcome I'm seeking." Notice again in paragraph 10a, Connors uses the phrase, "Well, the only thing that I'm interested in . . ." and in paragraph 12f-m, he talks about checking references and says, "I'd like to hear from some of your clients before I even spend any time talking with you. I can make the decisions based on what people tell me, and I would also like to see a list of clients that you've worked with." He continually refers to himself as making the decisions based on the input. Again in paragraph 16, he says, "I found that they could supply us with information. . . ."; notice the reference to "I" again.

Process Approach: More Options

Notice in paragraph 4a-b, Connors says, "Well, I'm going to change the policies around here." That indicates an individual who is open to change and will make changes based on the results of what the policies are presently producing. That indicates a More Options pattern, emphasizing that this would expand his possibilities (i.e., save him from these kinds of interruptions), where a Procedures person would be more concerned with the steps Susan had gone through. Also notice in paragraph 6, when Connors speaks he does not set up a system or procedure, he just says, "Well, you have that right." and the next time he speaks (paragraph 8), "Sure, go ahead. I have a few minutes." Both responses reflect a man who is not constrained by structure; he is really open to the possibilities. If someone were more Procedures oriented, they would indicate to the person calling an outline of what they would or wouldn't like. Notice in paragraph 12f-k, he does indicate some procedure by telling Susan that he would like to hear from some of the clients before he can even spend any time talking with her. This indicates that he does have some procedural sorting. The rating should be More Options rather than fully Options because Connors speaks first in an Options way and then identifies a Procedures sorting. In paragraph 16a-c, Connors answers the Motivating Source question, found in paragraph 15, with criteria yet begins by telling a short story ("Because after checking their references") that also indicates some Procedures sorting.

Convincer Strategy: Consistent

In paragraph 17d-i, Susan asks the question, "I'm curious, Mr. Connors, how often does the training company ... have to perform effectively for you before you're convinced that they can do a good job?" In paragraph 18a-b, Connors states, "... the fact is they have to do it every time." This indicates a Consistent Convincer Strategy. In other words, Connors has to be sold every time and will not recognize individual success until he has experienced it.

Process Relationship: Difference

In paragraph 23h-m, Susan asks the question, " . . . there is just one more question I would like to ask you, and that is what is the relationship between the type of training you used last year and the training that you used the year before?" In paragraph 24b-e, Connors states that it's totally different each year, which means that he sorts for difference first and notices value in things that change.

Process Scope: General

Notice in Connors's conversation that although he gives Susan some information, most of his statements tend to be more general, leaving Susan in the dark as to what specifically he would require from an outside training program. If you count the specific details in his speech, you will find almost none.

Decision Strategy: Auditory/Talk

In paragraph 19c-e, Susan asks the Decision Strategy question. In paragraph 20a-d, Connors says, "That's easy, you can hear the response of my people, and I could talk to each of them to be sure I was hearing right." The use of these words indicates that Connors's Decision Strategy is based on hearing from his people and talking.

HOS PROFILE CHART

Motivating Language/Criteria Words

_____

_____

_____

_____

_____

_____

_____

_____

Motivating Direction

Away From	More Away than Toward	Equally Away/Toward	More Toward than Away	Toward

Motivating Source

External	More External than Internal	Equally Ext/Int	More Internal than External	Internal

Process Approach

Options	More Options than Procedures	Equally Option/Proceed	More Procedures than Options	Procedures

Decision Strategy

Visual	Auditory	Feelings

Convincer Strategy

Automatic	Consistent	# of Examples	Period of Time

Process Scope

General	More General than Specific	Equally Gen/Spec	More Specific than General	Specific

Process Relationship

Same	Same/ Difference	Difference	Difference/ Same

Index